PERMISSION to NAP

Written especially for Linda Murphy

(as if she ever needed permission...)

D0507627

PERMISSION to NAP
Taking Time to Restore Your Spirit

JILL MURPHY LONG

SOURCEBOOKS, INC.®
NAPERVILLE, ILLINOIS

Published by Sourcebooks, Inc.
P.O. Box 4410, Naperville, Illinois 60567-4410
(630) 961-3900
FAX: (630) 961-2168
www.sourcebooks.com

Library of Congress Cataloging-in-Publication Data
Long, Jill Murphy.
    Permission to nap: taking time to restore your spirit/by Jill Murphy Long.
        p. cm.
Includes bibliographical references.
    ISBN 1-57071-938-1 (hardcover: alk. paper)
1. Stress management for women. 2. Naps (Sleep) I. Title.
    RA785 .L65 2002
    155.9'042'082—dc21

                                                                                2001006797

                        Printed and bound in China
            IM 10 9 8 7 6 5 4 3 2

DEDICATION

To my mother, Christine Joan Condeelis Murphy, who deserved a nap, to my sister, Amy Murphy, who practices regularly and introduced me to the peacefulness of yoga, to my daughter, Brittany Christine Long, who reminds me to take a nap, and to all the women who need to hear they have permission to nap—this book was written for you.

ACKNOWLEDGMENTS

First and foremost, I wish to thank my husband, Greg Scott Long, for giving me his unconditional love and the freedom to follow my dream; my father, William Richard Murphy Jr., for instilling the confidence at a young age to accomplish whatever I set my mind to; and my brother, Michael Todd Murphy, for being my primary competitor, challenging me to be all that I can be.

Thank you to my writing instructors, Mike Whitlow, Shelba Robison, and Marcia Cohen and to the members of my writing groups: Sandy Schneider, Ruth Duncan, Linda Blinn, Bea MacArthur, Sam McCarver, Leigh Heyer, Rod Vickery, Roger Coleman, Thad Mikols, Johnnie Lucero, Mary Massy, Dottie Para, Dwight Layton, Nancy Ako, and my webmaster, Derrek Schlottmann. Thank you for your support, wisdom, and laughter.

To all of the women who completed my napping survey and reviewed sample chapters, I thank you, in particular, Daria Murphy. To all my friends and family—you know who you are—thank you for your constant support.

Thank you, Chris Painter, library director at the Bud Werner Memorial Library in Steamboat Springs, Colorado, for helping me with historical and art research.

All my teachers throughout my life, including my yoga instructors and fellow yogis, a heartfelt thanks is offered.

To my agent, Elizabeth Pomada, who kept the faith, especially when the rejection letters kept landing on the desk; I thank you for finding Deb Werksman, my wonderful and insightful editor at Sourcebooks. Cheers, Elizabeth—you were right!

CONTENTS

INTRODUCTION

*We must learn to be still in the midst of activity
and to be vibrantly alive in repose.*
—Indira Gandhi (1917–1984)

I wrote this book because I saw how tired, frustrated, and depleted many women have become living their fast-paced lives. Our minds, bodies, and spirits require time to be quiet and still.

For many, relaxing is a difficult habit to develop; it goes against the niceties ingrained in us since we were first adorned in pink.

As part of my research for this book, I conducted a survey about napping among friends and business associates across the country. I asked them to tell me if they napped, how they accomplished it, and if they didn't—why not? The responses came in from more than one hundred and fifty career women, working mothers, stay-at-home moms, and wise women.

In handwritten notes, many women expressed frustration at having no time to nap. Others told me that they felt lazy if they put their feet up or had to be sick to relish a cup of tea and sit still for a while. Married women and mothers reported that their partners and/or children interrupted them. Many voiced there that was not a quiet place in the entire household to find tranquillity. And too many replied, "I'm just too busy to nap." Even though all of the women admitted to dreaming of time alone, only a few actually rested or napped daily.

Beginner's Mind by Amy Murphy

I wrote this book to help women slow their days and sit for a while. Whether they sleep or not, the downtime is essential. This is much more than just a book about naps—it is a book of discoveries, an introduction to elements to consider when creating a personal relaxation ritual. It is a source for expanding your spirit and doing what you know is good for you.

We all need a relaxation ritual. Your personal choice could be a twenty-minute nap, morning yoga to awaken the body and mind, a quiet session of walking meditation, or a little time sitting in nature—all can replenish the spirit.

We also need a place where we can go to rest—a nap sanctuary filled with soothing colors, comforting textures and fabrics, and calming aromatherapy to provide a serene haven, an oasis of comfort and beauty, a place of renewal and refreshment.

This self-care habit can provide the continual peacefulness that your spirit seeks and deserves. With a quiet respite secured in your hours, daily living can become much sweeter. Give this time as a gift to yourself. Consider this book a grant of permission—permission to rest, permission to pamper yourself, permission to nap.

Asleep among the Foxgloves
by Sidney Shelton

CHAPTER ONE

Women Who Nap Shamelessly

AND WITHOUT PERMISSION

It is good to have an end to journey towards; but it is the journey that matters in the end.
—*Ursula K. Le Guin (b.1929)*

When I started to write this book, everywhere I looked I saw signs to take a nap. In a national women's magazine, an alluring photo of an Adirondack chair placed pond-side with a frosted beverage beckoned the weary. A grocery store ad headline read: LYNN'S HAVING 50 GUESTS, A DELI TRAY, A FRUIT TRAY, A DESSERT TRAY AND ODDLY ENOUGH, A NAP. In a men's magazine, a two-page color ad provided a snapshot of what pure tranquillity looks like with a close-up of a young father and son napping in a hammock. The same year, *Real Simple* magazine was launched to extol the importance of living a calmer, more enriched, and balanced life.

For most women, however, the actual act of napping eludes us. Daily exhaustion and an urge for caffeine have nothing to do with age, but with how fast life is moving and the less-than-adequate sleep received each night. The body, a resilient system, can be recharged if given the chance, but women always have something else to do.

From the pages of art books, images of women relaxing persuade the harried to rest. Impressionist painter Berthe Morisot's *Young Girl Reclining* portrays the sweetness of sitting still, as does American-born Mary Cassatt's *Portrait of Lydia Cassatt, the Artist's Sister*.

Many female poets and authors illuminate the importance of relaxation as a part of every woman's daily life. Poet Emily Dickinson set an example for Victorian ladies and napped. Edith Wharton, Virginia Woolf, Isak Dinesen, Madeleine L'Engle, and Alice Walker all affirm a woman's decision to rest in their peaceful, yet convincing prose.

Decades of medical research maintain the body's need for at least eight hours of sleep per night to repair and regenerate for the new day. Sleep studies also reveal that the midday dip in energy is natural. When we respond with a siesta, we give our bodies a chance to destress.

CULTURAL SNAPSHOTS

... there is a luxury in being quiet in the heart of chaos.
—*Virginia Woolf (1882–1941)*

I spoke with international authors, business executives, and women from around the world and became more convinced that this venerable napping tradition of many cultures is a good, healthy habit—one

Americans should adopt for life. Ancient civilizations considered napping as normal as eating and drinking. Historians find traces of this daily habit as early as the fifth century B.C., when Asians, Athenians, Romans, and Egyptians delighted in the custom of afternoon sleep.

Today, Spain, Latin America, China, India, and parts of the Middle East are still big napping territories. Most Europeans—except the Germans, our forefathers of the Protestant work ethic— usually snooze or relax in the middle of the day. For the Chinese, the age-old custom of *xuixi*, which means "to rest", is practiced regardless of where they reside. If you try to reach a diplomat in the Chinese Embassy in Washington, D.C., between 12 and 2 P.M., they will be doing what they have always done at this time—napping.

In America, this act of self-care is all too often a luxury of the rich, the retired, kindergarten or college students, or an exception permitted when ill. This is something the American psyche desperately needs and wants. Women are the number one candidates for this well-deserved rest, but why aren't we napping yet?

WHERE ARE ALL THE NAPPING WOMEN?

In my country of origin, South America, I never felt guilty about napping.
In the United States, people think they should always be on the go.
—*Pilar Layton, mother, senior care residence administrator, Wagon Wheel, California*

Most American women feel guilty about taking time for themselves. Others are frustrated from being interrupted by everyone—husbands, kids, friends, family, and neighbors—when they try to make the time to be alone. Those who take naps reportedly have to protect their time and then justify why they were sleeping.

The bright side of my survey was from those who indulged regularly in beautiful naps or make time to do other spirit-settling activities. They celebrate with an elegant tea party for one, read inspirational quotes or affirmations, meditate, practice yoga, and sit and watch the afternoon sky. Some rely on soothing music or wrap up in a favorite blanket and do nothing but breathe. They have discovered how to quiet their busy worlds for a few precious moments every day. We should applaud those who have adopted this healthy habit into their lives and then we should decide to join them.

The Men vs. Women Nap Factor

Why do women tend to feel guilty about napping, but men do not?

—*Pam Lee, mother, high school English teacher, York, Pennsylvania*

Men have always created their own space without guilt and without permission. Albert Einstein and Thomas Edison frequently snoozed. Within the office of politics and world diplomacy, Sir Winston Churchill changed into his pajamas to nap and Charles V, the Holy Roman Emperor, also enjoyed his siestas. Presidents Johnson, Coolidge, Kennedy, Reagan, Clinton, and Bush Sr. and Jr. opted for regular afternoon shut-eye sessions to combat their demanding schedules. Leonardo da Vinci credited his increased creativity to the influence of a midday doze. Johannes Brahms purportedly worked on his famous lullaby around his nap each day.

As our world moves faster, women keep adding more to their lives. Ozzie and Harriet are no longer the rule—in fact, they are fossils. Today's Harriet endures a mad dash to the daycare center five days a week. Another source of stress is lack of help around the house. Domestic duties still fall disproportionately into the woman's lap, even if both partners put in full-time hours at the office and this same uneven housework scenario occurs with or without children. The man around the house now picks up after himself better, but only contributes up to 22 percent of the housework, the dishes, the laundry, the grocery shopping, and the meal preparation.

Moms run on overdrive every day. It is no wonder that the number of women suffering from burnout is on the rise. In her attempt to do it all, superwoman has perfected squeezing more time out of the day by sleeping less, but how long will her energy and spirit last?

UNDERSTANDING THE NEED FOR GOOD SLEEP

Every person, especially every woman, should be alone sometime
during the year, some part of each week, and each day.
—*Anne Morrow Lindbergh (1906–2001)*

She's busy. He's busy. We are busy all the time and connected via cell phone, pager, and email. There used to be a quiet moment on a long flight, but not anymore, thanks to the addition of sky phones. Now you are never out of touch—except with yourself. In our Puritan-rooted society, it is our *busyness* that we, and others, value as our worth. We brag about the few hours of sleep on which we can function, yet we fight the urge to nap. This yawning majority now wears their badges of sleepiness like status symbols, but by mid afternoon, many stumble around the office and at home with heavy eyelids.

Since Thomas Edison invented the light bulb in 1879, nighttime sleep for the average American has dropped from nine hours per night to less than seven.

We are sleep cheats and are beginning to pay the price. Napping needs to be made a respectable part of the American day; the thinking that equates naps with indolence, old age, or preschoolers must be dismissed as passé and the guilt surrounding this act of self-preservation erased. An afternoon siesta, rich in the most restful phase of slow-wave sleep, is a very effective tool for regaining productivity and balance in life. If we would only take the time to stop our minds from racing from one thought to the next and rest tired bodies, our systems would recharge. We need to recognize this habit as a good health measure.

We cut into our nighttime sleep to do it all and, as a result, the consequences of sleeplessness begin to appear: irritability, weight gain or loss, depression, premature aging, chilliness, lethargy, and insomnia. Our creativity wanes. Our sense of humor is lost. We cannot cope well with the demands of daily life. We find ourselves living in a state of constant exhaustion.

What type of life are we leading? Are these tasks—the ones we put first in our days—even conscious choices? Are they more important than sleep? Are they more imperative than our health?

MAKING TIME

Beside the noble art of getting things done, there is the noble art of leaving things undone. The wisdom of life consists in the elimination of nonessentials.
—Lin Yutang (1895–1976)

The Zen concept of "mindfulness" is the act of having complete concentration in the moment. In mindfulness, you focus on now. There is no future, no past. For many women, who have less time to do everything, including sleep, this concept appears to be a lovely but fleeting impossibility. Yet mindfulness is very simple and very effective. If doing the dishes, just do the dishes. If resting, just rest. If you are writing a brief, just write the brief. Cease all other activities. Focus on the activity or task at hand to feel at peace, rather than starting ten other things and feeling frazzled.

As you prepare to relax or work, say one word aloud repeatedly that describes what you plan to do. Gather your blanket and book and say, "Rest, rest…" In the morning, when you set up your desk, say, "Write, write…" This process of verbalizing the activity or task readies the mind for acceptance. You will also feel a comforting sensation encompass you, a feeling of being less rushed, less stressed.

Practice mindfulness in your everyday life. Make shorter lists of what should be done today. If you do not accomplish some of them, simply move them to tomorrow or later in the week. Be sure to put at least one relaxing activity in your day. Congratulate yourself on all of your daily accomplishments, no matter how few or small.

Practice mindfulness in a relaxation ritual. Seek stillness and listen to your thoughts. Surround yourself regularly in this pure, sweet solitude. Make time for such simple pleasures as a nap, a walk, or daydreaming. A nap will feed your mind, body, and spirit so you can return to your day renewed and refreshed.

Success in mastering something new always begins with small steps. On your journey of discovery, may peace always be your companion. Try any of these self-care acts and start your practice of mindfulness today.

DRAW A BUBBLE BATH AND SOAK IN THE
ILLUMINATION OF A DOZEN MINI ROSE-SCENTED CANDLES.

WRAP UP IN A CHERISHED ROBE AND SIT FOR A
WHILE WITH YOUR EYES CLOSED IN YOUR FAVORITE CHAIR.

TOSS A QUILT ON THE GROUND.
LIE DOWN ON YOUR BACK, STARE AT THE SKY, AND JUST BREATHE.

SETTLE DOWN WITH A PHOTO ALBUM.
PAGE THROUGH THE MEMORIES AND COUNT SMILES.

SIP A CUP OF HERBAL TEA BEFORE A SMALL CANDLE.
WATCH ITS FLAME AND BE MESMERIZED BY ITS DANCE OF FIRE.

STROLL AROUND THE BLOCK AND MARVEL AT
HOW NATURE BRAVELY MIXES COLORS TOGETHER.

CURL UP WITH A BOOK OF POETRY. READ A PASSAGE ALOUD.
TASTE THE TANG OF EVERY WORD. THEN CLOSE YOUR
EYES FOR A FEW MINUTES AND REVEL IN THE POETRY OF SILENCE.

In your relaxation time, search for simplicity. This piece of tranquillity carved from a busy day is the most precious and important gift that you can give yourself. You deserve a nap. You are not being selfish. You have earned this peace.

GIRL UNDER A PARASOL
BY PEDRO LIRA

CHAPTER TWO

The Truth about Napping

TODAY AND TOMORROW

Knowing that naps are great for your heart allows me to lie down without guilt,
wrap myself in cotton, and languish in the healing power of sleep.
—*Gail McMeekin, author of* The 12 Secrets of Highly Creative Women *(b.1951)*

Being well rested is crucial for productivity, essential for good health, and may be the basis for happiness. As we mature, our lives change, and therefore, our sleep patterns are affected. College students actually need up to ten hours of sleep a night. New parents lose from four hundred to seven hundred and fifty hours of sleep during the first year with a newborn under their roof. La Leche League, the support group for nursing mothers, recommends that all new moms take a nap whenever the baby sleeps.

According to a recent survey by the National Sleep Foundation, 74 percent
of women still get less sleep per night than men.

As our bodies grow older, we may wake up more often during the night, but this is because our lighter stages of sleep increase while our deeper stages decrease—not because we need less sleep. No matter what age we are, twenty-five to ninety-five, we still require at least the minimum recommended eight hours of sleep and all adults can benefit from a nap.

Our bodies have an internal clock known as a circadian rhythm that signals us when it is time to sleep. This is why we feel a drop in energy at night and another dip during the daytime between 1 and 4 P.M. The tired feeling you experience after lunch is not due to a big meal or alcohol, but rather to the dip in your rhythm. You feel sleepy because your body needs and wants to rest.

Sleep experts recommend keeping afternoon siestas under one and a half hours, so as not to interfere with nighttime sleep. For most people, a snooze of fifteen to thirty minutes is best. Experiment to see what works for you.

In a world that never shuts down, many people brag: As soon as my head hits the pillow, I'm gone. Unfortunately, this is the equivalent of someone saying that he or she is a good eater and as soon as he or she sits down to dinner, the food is gone in under a minute. This is not the sign of a good eater, but of someone who is famished. The same is true for those who fall asleep so fast. If you fall asleep quickly, take a look at how sleep deprived your body may truly be. Tally your sleep hours to make sure you are getting enough ZZZs time. The numbers do not lie.

The National Commission on Sleep Disorders estimates that sixty million Americans are chronically sleep-deprived and claims this condition is perhaps one of the biggest health problems plaguing our society today.

The list of side effects due to being sleep deprived is long. You may experience short-term memory loss, a decrease in alertness and hand-eye coordination, and a sense of overall fatigue. If you continually cut into your sleep time, your habit can cause premature aging. Chilliness, due to poor circulation, is the result of the body not being provided enough time to repair itself. The first hour of our nighttime sleep is the most important because this is when the body circulates the human growth hormone to repair and rebuild. The same effect is gained with a nap as the body experiences the same deep sleep.

According to Stanley Coren, Ph.D., professor of psychology at the University of British Columbia and the author *of Sleep Thieves: An Eye-Opening Exploration into the Science and Mysteries of Sleep*, the accidents at Three-Mile Island, the Challenger shuttle explosion, Chernobyl, and the Exxon Valdez oil spill were all attributable to "severely sleep-deprived personnel who rotated shifts, or held down long hours without sleeping. Internal clocks were out of alignment with the activity and alertness required for the jobs, resulting in exhaustion and crew fatigue."

We must begin to value sleep as much as eating well and exercising regularly.

Getting to bed an hour earlier and including a siesta in your daily routine can help to erase sleep debt. If you are getting adequate sleep, a short doze can add an extra surge of energy and creativity to your afternoon. This spring, set the example in your household and neighborhood and take part in the National Sleep Awareness Week sponsored by the National Sleep Foundation in Washington, D.C. Since 1998, this campaign has encouraged Americans to get to bed earlier the week before daylight savings time. Come Monday morning, there will be one less sleepyhead driving to work.

Our bodies know when to stop. We need to listen, but most of us are moving too fast to hear or see any signs as serious. Give yourself permission to say, "No" to more to do and, "Yes" to sleep and a daily doze. Your body will thank you with a burst of extra energy and a clearer and calmer mind upon awakening.

NAPS—SUDDENLY IN VOGUE

We must pull in for short moments to take care of ourselves, then we can return to the people and places of our lives renewed, refreshed, and ready to continue…

—*Chris Casson Madden*

"Napping should not be frowned upon at the office or make you feel guilty (when) at home," says Dr. James B. Maas, a psychologist and sleep expert at Cornell. "It should have the status of daily exercise."

Slowly but steadily, U.S. companies are incorporating nap facilities into the workplace. According to the National Sleep Foundation, 16 percent of those surveyed said their employers allow naps, but it is a big secret who is actually allowed to snooze at work. Napping on the U.S. corporate front is a quiet, but growing revolution.

Napping at Home

Naps are refreshing, a delicious escape.

—Denise Meyer, mother, realtor, Pinetop, Arizona

Mothers at home with young children also deserve the equivalent of a power nap. Join your toddlers at two in the afternoon and accomplish only rest. You will be more energetic when you awaken and able to tackle what seemed like a mountain an hour ago.

To get started on working and living a healthier life, promise yourself one respite a week. Once you get used to taking time for yourself to rest, you may find yourself looking forward to this new addition to your routine.

THE SOUL OF THE ROSE
BY JOHN WILLIAM WATERHOUSE

CHAPTER THREE

Because I Want To

AND OTHER READILY AVAILABLE ANSWERS

The beginning of health is sleep.

—Irish proverb

Our environment at work, and sometimes at home, no longer exposes us to the seasonal changes in light and dark. Our bodies have forgotten what is true day and night. Over the course of a lifetime, the benefits of a good night's sleep and a daily nap far outweigh the extra hours picked up by cutting into our sleep time. The next time you are asked, "Why are you napping?" give any of the following five reasons.

1. TO INCREASE MY CREATIVITY

There is no point at which you can say, "Well, I'm successful now. I might as well take a nap."

—Carrie Fisher (b. 1956)

The act of creation and discovery takes time and a calm environment. Sir Isaac Newton was not running around with a cell phone and beeper when he discovered the law of gravity. He was sitting under a tree.

2. FOR A STRONGER BODY

I'm at the point where my body and mind need that afternoon nap.
So why fight it? I look at it as my daily way to be nice to myself.
—Lisbeth Tanz-Harrison, mother, life coach, St. Louis, Missouri

Professional sport teams have a curfew. College students on athletic scholarship must be in by the witching hour. Athletes know. Coaches know. Sports trainers know and now you know, too. Adequate sleep every night and a daily doze will make you stronger.

In Great Britain, a study showed that weight lifters that were limited
to three hours of sleep a night for three days could not complete the
set numbers of curls, presses, and lifts by the second night.

3. TO FIGHT ILLNESS

A study from the University of California at San Diego showed that healthy men
who missed five hours of sleep produced fewer disease-fighting immune cells.

Did you know that the common cold lingers or the flu hits because of a weakened immune system due to sleep deprivation? People who suffer from poor sleep also show a reduction in

T-cell production, which makes the body more susceptible to infection. As you sleep, disease-fighting immune cells are produced to keep your immune system strong. Think about the last time that you were sick. What was your sleep like the week or two prior to becoming ill? Shoot for eight hours and fortify your health with a nap.

4. TO BOOST MY ENERGY

When I don't get enough sleep and start to get grouchy,
I realize it's time for my power nap.

—*Debbie Grove, mother, special education secretary, Shrewsbury, Pennsylvania*

Does a fog of drowsiness surround you during most afternoons? A short doze delivers a natural boost of energy without the crash later caused by the sugar or caffeine from soft drinks or coffee. If you cannot get a nap in your schedule tomorrow, go to bed a half hour earlier to achieve similar results. Unfortunately, tacking this extra time onto your morning sleep will not deliver the same benefit. Remember, it is the first hour of sleep, whether it is a nap or nighttime sleep, that gives your body the energy it needs.

5. FOR A LONGER LIFE

Longevity may be the best reason to spend one third of your life in bed. William Dement, M.D., Ph.D., director of the Stanford Sleep Disorder Clinic and chairman of the National Commission on Sleep Disorders Research, says, "Healthy sleep has been proven to be the single most important determinant in predicting longevity, more influential than diet, exercise, or heredity."

CREATE A RELAXATION RITUAL

We do not remember days, we remember moments.

—*Cesare Pavese (1908–1950)*

Memories of birthdays, weddings, anniversaries, and other celebrations add fulfillment to our lives. We can learn much from these rituals of life. Borrow from these precious moments and create a relaxation ritual of your own.

When entering your nap sanctuary, be sure to slow your movement. Stop time and hold it in your hands. Focus on nothing else except yourself. Right now at this moment, you deserve to be the center of attention. These moments are meant to be a celebration of you. The memory of these quiet times, with a distinct taste of peace, will linger and remind you to return again—and soon.

DESIGN A NAP SANCTUARY

Ah, but in such matters, it is only the first step that is difficult.

—*Madame Du Deffand (1697–1780)*

With any new endeavor, it is sometimes easier to stay with a program if you have a place to go. Design your own nap sanctuary to help your restorative habit grow stronger. Decide on an area in your home, be it a corner or an entire room, that can be set up for you and only you.

Decorate the room with items of comfort: a reclining chair, a blanket, a pillow, soft lighting, and perhaps a fountain. Organize a basket or box with napping items that you already own: incense or room spray, pajamas, slippers, an eye mask, and a book of inspirational quotations. Occasionally, add a new indulgence such as a feather pillow, a lap robe, or a scented candle.

To keep your nap routine fresh, change it from time to time. As summer returns, claim a nap spot outdoors. Hang up a hammock and treat yourself to an elegant glass of sparkling mineral water with a twist. As the winds begin to cool, unpack the warmest comforter you own and serve yourself a mug of hot apple cider. Each time you rest, congratulate yourself with a toast to your new healthy habit.

DISCOVER YOUR IDEAL NAPTIME

I'm a weekend napper. Saturday and Sunday are made for napping and I enjoy it.
—Liz Norwood, mother, account executive, Bothell, Washington

According to the University of California at Berkeley's *Wellness Letter*, the best time to nap is eight hours after waking up and eight hours before nighttime sleep. For example, if you wake at 6 A.M. and go to bed at 10 P.M., then 2:00 in the afternoon is your ideal time to nap. Be flexible with your naptime and plan to snooze anytime within one and a half hours of your optimal time. Once you have calculated your ideal time, block it off in your calendar and make it a date.

In the nap survey, some women said they indulged in longer naps of up to one and a half hours. Extra busy women reported that short siestas of fifteen to thirty minutes worked well for them. Discover what works best for you.

To counter the grogginess, keep your naps to twenty minutes or less. Sleep experts called this sensation *sleep inertia* or *post nap inertia*. This "sleep hangover" should pass after a few minutes. However, it is a fact that naps of two hours or longer can bring on this effect and may disturb nighttime sleep, so time your siesta accordingly.

NAP SECRETS

1. Feet up, please. Prone is the optimal position.

2. Order a dose of peace and quiet. Close the door. Turn off the lights, phone, and pager. If there is too much daylight to sleep, cover the window with a blanket, towel, or black-out shade. You can also opt for a scented eye cover, instead.

3. Be comfortable. Slip into pajamas, or at work, loosen any tight clothing and remove your shoes. Cover yourself with a blanket.

4. Keep it short. Rest for at least fifteen minutes, but aim for half an hour.

5. Do not watch the time. Turn the clock around or put your watch in a drawer.

6. Create a nap spot and fill it with a few items for comfort.

7. Keep it cool. Your nap area should be kept between sixty and sixty-five degrees Fahrenheit.

8. Let go of stress. Use a handy "to do" pad to jot down key words to remind you of what to do later and then hide the paper. Do not leave it by your head and continue to let your concerns bother you.

9. Pamper your body. Yoga, a bath, or a massage can help you relax and fall asleep.

10. Breathe! Start your quiet time with meditation, guided imagery, or deep-breathing exercises.

11. Watch out for stimulants. Caffeine is found in chocolate, cocoa, cola sodas, in some uncolas like Mountain Dew, and in over-the-counter medicines such as headache remedies, diuretics, diet aids, and pain relievers that can contain as much caffeine as a cup of

coffee. If swallowed at the prescribed times, the doses could equal up to six cups of coffee throughout the day. Nicotine also is a powerful stimulant.

12. Enjoy teatime. Before naptime, treat yourself to a relaxing cup of herbal tea, or when you awaken, as a reward, have ready a tall, iced beverage. Most herbal infusions are caffeine-free and green tea only has about 35 milligrams of caffeine.

13. Move your body regularly. Exercise is a great stress buster and mind sharpener, and is guaranteed to give you more energy. In addition to making you feel better, "playing" will help you sleep better, too.

14. Say yes to pasta. At lunch, eat foods high in carbohydrates. Whole grains, breads, and pasta raise the level of serotonin in the brain, which creates a calming effect on the body and can make napping easier. Peanuts, bananas, and sunflower seeds—foods rich in B vitamins—can counteract the effects of stress and help you doze better.

15. Book it. Schedule a nap as a personal care appointment. Think of your nap as a meeting with an important client. Do not cancel.

16. "Way to go!" Every time you put your feet up, congratulate yourself. Positive reinforcement ensures your healthy habit will be repeated tomorrow.

17. Be ready. When traveling or for the office, pack a nap-in-a-bag. If at home, first thing in the morning, set up a relaxation corner to entice you to rest later in the day.

18. Easy does it. Wake up slowly with a few neck rolls or gentle stretches so as not to shock the nervous system and undermine the benefits of your beautiful nap. Resume your day in an unhurried manner.

PERMISSION TO NAP

The beginning is always today.

—*Mary Wollstonecraft (1759–1797)*

Most of the time, unnecessary self-restrictions and false burdens keep us from the peaceful times the spirit yearns for and deserves. Make the change in your life to carve out your own personal time and space. With a little ingenuity, a bit of preplanning, and perhaps rearranging, anywhere you can put your feet up will work beautifully.

Give yourself permission to stop a task or eliminate a commitment before you introduce a new element into your day. This rule applies even when you grant yourself the time to do nothing. Subtract a "to do" from your list, so you can relax peacefully. This serenity is truly what you need. Give yourself permission to nap today.

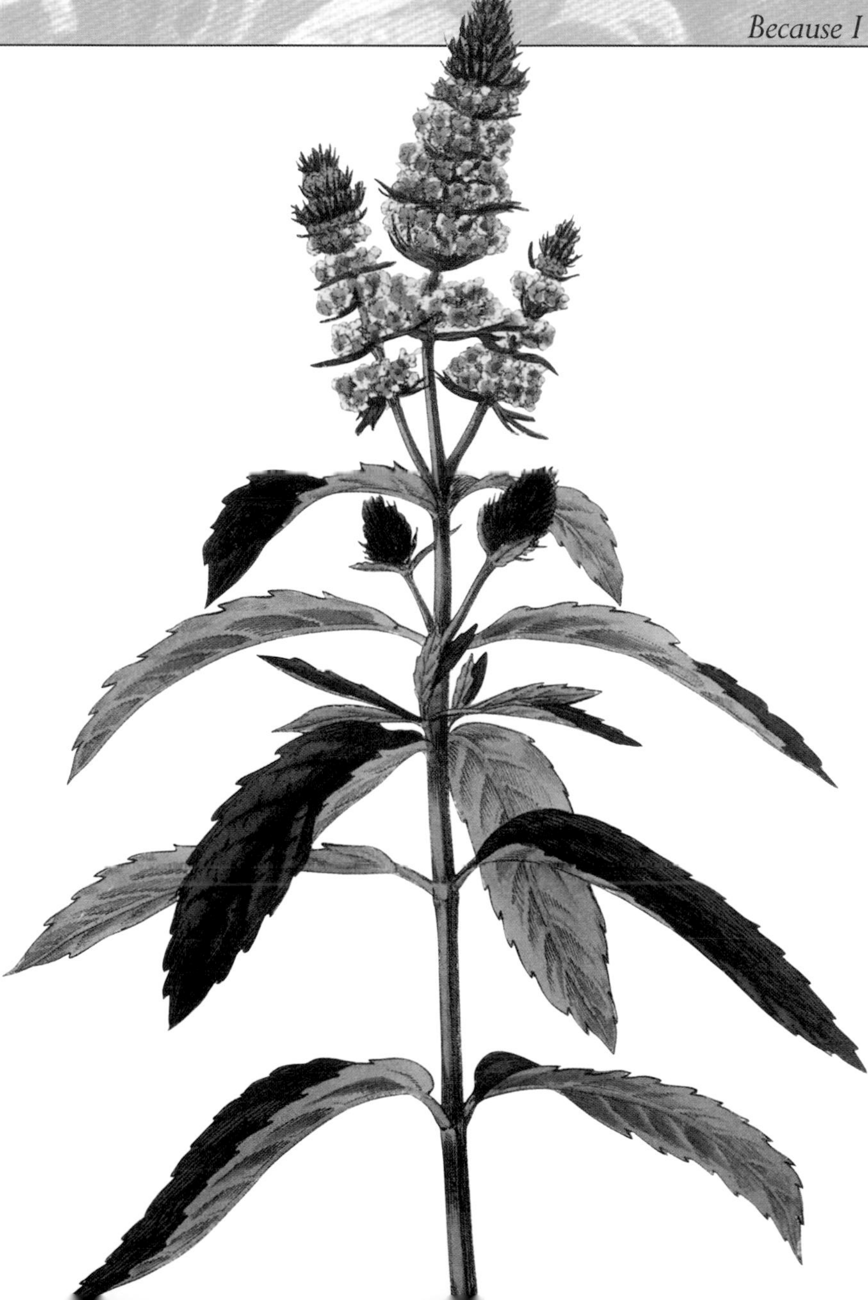

The Betrothed
By John William Godward

CHAPTER FOUR

Seasonal Escapes at Home

LUXURIOUS NAP RECIPES

Dolce far niente! *(How sweet it is to do nothing!)*
—*Italian saying*

These twelve luxurious recipes will show how your nap can be a true indulgence. If you do not have any of the items mentioned, use your imagination and substitute what is readily available. Any soothing music, beverage, tactile accessory, aromatherapy, essential oil, or object of beauty can bring peace to your day.

Cut a rose from your garden or ask a neighbor if you may select a single stem from his. Scent any pillow by spraying it lightly with a homemade mixture of an essential oil and water. Borrow your child's blanket or your partner's sweatshirt. Play your favorite slow, instrumental music. Pour a refreshing glass of water and garnish it with whatever fruit or vegetable is in the refrigerator.

Do and use whatever slows your mind and body. Your spirit will thank you. May these suggestions spark your creativity to design even more beautiful naps for future afternoons spent in pure bliss.

January: *Winter Haven*

hot cocoa with marshmallows and whipped cream

wool blanket and pillows

essential oil of clary sage

The Isle of Dreaming **by Kate Price**

Fooling with Words: A Collection of Poets and Their Craft **by Bill D. Moyers**

Wailing winds, gray as the winter's sky, cold as the frozen ground, drift snow across driveways. In more than half of the fifty states, this is interpreted as the perfect time to snooze. If it is not snowing where you live, borrow the northerners' excuse. This afternoon, decide to be a guest in your own home.

Shake open a blanket, perhaps woven in the true colors of the Scottish highland—moss, slate, and heather. For extra comfort, add more pillows and maybe include a neck roll pillow, too. To clear the air and your mind, dot a ceramic light bulb ring with essential oil of clary sage. Turn on the light and wait for its alluring essence to cross the room to you. Sit and listen to a musical tapestry as the soft sounds of a dulcimer and cello serenade your soul with melodies from yesteryear. Within moments, you will be drifting on ethereal clouds, far above the forever-green fields of Scotland.

Afterward, treat yourself to a cup of sinfully rich, heartwarming cocoa. Extend the afternoon a little longer and read a few tender pages of poetry. You have earned these extra minutes of solitude. Indulge all month long.

God made the world round so we could never be able to see too far down the road.
—Isak Dinesen (1885–1962)

FEBRUARY: *Far East Daydream*

jasmine green tea with honey

bolster and boudoir pillows

frankincense essential oil

The Ultimate Massage and Relaxation **by Miramar**

Stumbling toward Enlightenment **by Geri Larkin**

While February might be reserved for lovers, it is also a good month to take special care of your self. Design a relaxation sanctuary worthy of an empress. Start on your journey to a quieter place by brewing Japanese green tea. For a joyful taste of nature, lace your steaming beverage with a drop of wild honey.

Scattered pillows on the floor are an invitation to sit cross-legged and serenely sip your hot beverage. Let your body succumb to the consoling tonic. From a diffuser, essential oil of frank-incense sends its woodsy aroma to every corner and creates a peaceful setting ideal for your restorative time. Allow calming instrumentals to ready your mind and body for a nap. Nestle in among the pillows and read an enlightening story.

When finished with your tea and book, lie back on the floor with your feet rolled out and hands opened by your side. This yoga position is a resting pose called *savasana*. Close your eyes. Scan your body for tight spots where stress has its hold. Let your entire body melt into the floor.

Inhale through your nose to a slow count of four. Hold. Now exhale through your nose to a count of eight. Do this several times to relax your body. Be mindful of the moment. Keep your thoughts focused on your breathing. Treasure this precious time spent in total tranquillity. When you awaken, return to your day in a slow manner so that the feeling of peace stays in your spirit.

Something that we think is impossible now is not impossible in another decade.
—Constance Baker Motley (b. 1921)

MARCH: *Spa Time*

sparkling mineral water with berries and a sprig of mint

chenille blanket, spa robe, and slippers

electric aromatherapy diffuser filled with lavender beads

Water Circles **by Mia Jang**

Art and Love: An Illustrated Anthology of Love Poetry **by Kate Farrell**

Today, focus on today. To begin your time in serenity, write all worries on a piece of paper and slip it into a drawer. In an hour, you can go back to what needs to be done, but for now, promise that all of your thoughts will be centered on your well-being. It is a new month and time to create a new relaxation sanctuary.

All spas offer patrons a lovely beverage to sip while relaxing; make your haven no exception. Pour sparkling mineral water into a fancy flute and release a few berries into the bubbly water. Float a sprig of mint on the water's transparent surface. Sit a while and watch the effervescent beverage. Bring it close to your face and feel its fine mist like a mini facial. Breathe in its sweet aroma to refresh your spirit.

Next, surround yourself in the subtle aroma of a relaxing essence. Place a dish of lavender buds nearby, or if you have an electric diffuser, add lavender beads to summon sleep.

Slip into a plush robe and a pair of your favorite slippers. Select a thick, warm blanket of chenille or mohair and drape it over your prized nap seat. Finally, turn the songs of tranquillity on low to complete your new home spa. Gently cover yourself with the blanket and relax. Sip your beverage and then sleep for twenty minutes. When you awaken, take a few minutes to page through an art book. You will feel full of energy and a compassion for all.

> *By shallow rivers, to whose falls melodious birds sing madrigals.*
> —Christopher Marlowe (1564–1593)

APRIL: *Gentle Rains*

Earl Grey tea and sugar cubes
faux fur blanket
fragrant waters with neroli essential oil
The Mask and Mirror **by Loreena McKennitt**
French Lessons **by Peter Mayle**

When rain gently blankets the glass pane and makes the entire world outside seem like a misty dream, open the window and catch a few drops in your palm. The first warm shower of the season begins the time of rebirth with its signs of new life everywhere. Leave the window ajar and let fresh air into the house. This afternoon, a delicate cup of Earl Grey, a classic and excellent tea, is yours. Sweeten the moment and drop in a sugar cube or two. Close your eyes as the essence of bergamot oil, a strong aroma of citrus, rises from the steam, showing you why this tea has been wildly popular since the 1800s. If you are caffeine-sensitive, you may want to treat yourself to tea after your nap or purchase decaffeinated Earl Gray, but if your snooze is to be a short one, the trace amount should not affect your afternoon sleep.

Add another layer of ambiance with five drops of neroli essential oil added to a bowl of hot water placed nearby. The fragrance of sweet orange blossom will soon fill the air.

On any monochromatic day, lift your mood by covering yourself with a decadent blanket such as a faux fur of mink, sable, or leopard. Wrap its warmth completely around your body and be still.

Read one short essay, which is guaranteed to transport you to Provence, France. Afterwards, close your eyes. Mystic music from northern lands plays softly in the background and paints a pleasant dreamscape. Its comforting harmonies whisper, "Sleep…" and you listen.

> *Comes the fresh spring in all her green completed.*
> —*Elizabeth Barrett Browning (1806–1861)*

MAY: *Everyday Peace*

spring water with slices of cucumber and orange

handwoven blanket, a dream pillow, and bare feet

bouquet of fragrant roses

Everyday Serenity: Meditation for People Who Do Too Much **by David Kundtz**

Proclaim the next thirty days a tribute to you and mark the start of your celebration with a dozen roses. This "queen of all flowers" is often a repeating element in art and poetry. Decide that your life is art and you are entitled to such a colorful bouquet. Announce the official changing of your nap sanctuary from indoors to outdoors by placing your vase of buds under a market umbrella or in another shady spot.

Collect about you a few nap essentials. Choose a handwoven Native American or Mexican blanket or an incredibly soft, knitted throw with six-inch fringe—any favorite tactile comfort will do—in case a breeze should kick up. Extra pillows or a dream pillow will make your new spot even more heavenly.

In a glass pitcher filled with ice and water, float thinly sliced cucumbers and orange pinwheels until its surface resembles a cool, abstract masterpiece of secondary hues. Cover the pitcher with a lid, use a tea towel, or see if you can find one of those ingenious pitchers with a coordinated glass that also serves as a lid. A sip of this surprisingly refreshing beverage will remind your body that it is time to relax. Take a book with you for pondering after your siesta.

Come to your peaceful time just as you are. Today, your nap attire is whatever you are wearing sans shoes and socks. With your eyes closed, sit a moment outdoors. Be still in mind. Be still in body. Thank yourself for this time to luxuriate in complete comfort and the opportunity to do absolutely nothing—without guilt.

Life is either a daring adventure or nothing at all.
—Helen Keller (1880–1968)

JUNE: *Hammock Afternoons*
fruity beverage
outside pajamas and sandals
hammock and pillow
sandalwood incense stick
Guided Meditation for Stress **by Compass Productions**

The season of summer has finally arrived in all its shining triumph and glory. Time spent in nature is truly wonderful for the spirit. Welcome these carefree, precious days and doze outdoors as often as you can.

To kick off this summertime nap, first browse through your kitchen or dining room cabinets and select whatever stemware fits your carefree disposition today. Choose a cocktail glass, an oversized mug, a delicate teacup, or even a small bowl to give your respite a new spin. Try fresh-squeezed orange juice in a purple wine goblet or a banana-pineapple-coconut smoothie served in a red martini glass.

Change into your relaxation attire: a loose, lightweight dress or drawstring cotton pants with a T-shirt can pass for outdoor pajamas. Wear sandals, but plan to remove them immediately once prone.

Stroll outside to your reserved corner. Stretch out on a beach towel or in a hammock if you own one. Now is the time to claim your new spot for the summer. Take in a deep breath of serenity. Savor the fresh scent of the lush, blossoming earth. Signal the start of your relaxation ritual by lighting a stick of sandalwood incense to complement the natural aromas of nature.

This afternoon, use meditation exercises and lift the stress from your body. Listen carefully to the instructions and let your mind travel without any baggage. These are the moments to appreciate: time for yourself, time to be still, and time to take a beautiful nap.

I only know that summer sang to me.
—Edna St. Vincent Millay (1892–1950)

JULY: *Summer Forever Days*

iced secha tea with raw sugar crystals

silk sheet

ceramic amphora with essential oil of ylang ylang

Seascapes Piano Solos **by Michael Jones**

Gift from the Sea **by Anne Morrow Lindbergh**

The heat of the day has already climbed far above the predicted temperatures; even the flowers in the garden hide from the sun's harsh rays. Acknowledge the fact that this type of afternoon is best only for resting. In front of the fan, place a big bowl filled with ice cubes. The instant cold air across your face will be a welcome relief. Find a silk or other extra-soft sheet and place it in your sanctuary. Pull on appropriate daytime slumber wear, anything loose and cool, like an oversized sleep shirt or a summer nightgown. Fill a ceramic amphora with the relaxing essential oil of ylang ylang. Its tropical fragrance will soon perfume the air.

With nature music on low, belly flop across the bed. Do not move around because that only stirs up the sultry air. Turn to a dog-eared page and visit this favorite author again. In a whisper, read a passage to yourself. Close the book. Close your eyes. Visualize the whelk shell the writer has described. From this balmy destination, sleep beckons. Go. When you awaken, you will be refreshingly cool.

There shall be eternal summer in the grateful heart.
—*Celia Laighton Thaxter (1835–1894)*

AUGUST: *Personal Time*

lemonade with lime slices

fragrant bath with eucalyptus essential oil

Barcelona Nights **by Ottmar Liebert**

A Room of Her Own: Women's Personal Spaces **by Chris Casson Madden**

Since this is the month when everyone else is on vacation, decide to take additional time to pamper yourself. Declare today a personal day. This afternoon, stretch time and include a luxurious bath prior to your nap.

Begin in the kitchen and create a new beverage concoction. Get creative and blend up a smoothie with any frozen fruit you may have or serve good old lemonade in a margarita glass with a lime slice anchored on its sugared rim. Try a champagne glass filled to the top with carbonated mineral water and garnished with a maraschino cherry or a kiwi slice. Place your enticing drink within reach of the tub.

On the bed, leave the book that you plan to page through later and toss an extra sheet beside it. Select your favorite robe and change into it. Draw a tepid bath, mixing eight drops of eucalyptus essential oil under the spout. Stir well, so as not to leave red marks on your skin. The properties of this refreshing essential oil will cool your body temperature and make it easier to fall asleep. Invite the melodious rhythm of classical guitar into your relaxation haven and then step into the fragrant waters. Promise yourself that you will stay here until your fingertips wrinkle.

Upon exiting the spirit-soothing waters, enter the second phase of your relaxation ritual *au naturel*. Curl up with a book and cover with the sheet. Enjoy this mini vacation. Your calm body will thank you.

The very least you can do in your life is to figure what you hope for.

And the most you can do is live inside that hope.

—Barbara Kingsolver (b. 1955)

SEPTEMBER: *Indian Summer Escape*

orange-apple herbal tea with an orange slice and a stick of rock candy

knitted blanket

potted rose-scented geraniums

Passion Flute **by Stephen DeRuby**

The Book of Tea **by Kakuzo Okakura**

There is a slight change in the air; summer is beginning to fade, kids are back in school, yet the days seem as if they could go on forever. Now is the time to take a half hour for yourself.

Carry a small pot of tea and its accoutrements to your favorite outdoor spot. Stir your hot beverage with a stick of rock candy and let a slice of orange float on top. As you sip, enjoy the intermingling of sweetness plus a hint of citrus tartness. Through an opened window, tranquil music drifts out to meet you.

Close your eyes and imagine that you are deep within a forest. Breathe deeply and let the peace of nature embrace you. After your guided imagery session, open your eyes and treat yourself to a natural burst of aromatherapy. Pull your chair closer to the rose-scented geraniums or other fragrant flowers. Pick up a classic book and learn something new. Travel in your dreams to the described destination on the pages and see, hear, and taste the faraway culture of the new land.

Autumn is a second spring when every leaf is a flower.
—*Albert Camus (1913–1960)*

OCTOBER: *Autumn Color Retreat*

hot, spiced apple cider with a cinnamon stick

handmade quilt

homemade aromatherapy candle

Portraits on the Piano **by Mary Martin Stockdale**

The Prophet **by Kahlil Gibran**

When the leaves begin to turn colors and the wind blows a bit chilly, step outside into the crisp air with a quilt or other cherished blanket over your shoulder and a book under one arm. With a mug of hot, spiced apple cider in hand, twirl a stick of cinnamon into the honey-colored treat and sink into any available chair, swinging or reclining.

Create your own aromatherapy candle by adding six drops of essential oil to an unscented tea candle. Light your new scented candle and float it in a short vase or small bowl of water. The aroma should last the length of your nap session. Listen as piano solos sing like the wind through the treetops. Let your eyes close and imagine that you are lying beneath the canopy of trees. After your beautiful nap, start a book that you have vowed to read this year. Slowly, return to your day and continue to relish the sense of peace that your time alone has given you.

Happiness is not a state to arrive at, but a manner of traveling.
—*Margaret Lee Runbeck (1905–1956)*

NOVEMBER: *Rainy Day Respite*

red mellow bush herbal tea with 100 percent natural rooibos

feather bed and fleece blanket

potpourri with chamomile essential oil

indoor fountain

Women's Lip: Outrageous, Irreverent and Just Plain Hilarious Quotes
edited by Roz Warren

A light rain is released quietly from a gray sky. Raindrops patter on autumn leaves scattered all over the lawn. Raking must wait for a drier day. This moody weather is the perfect enticement to nap.

Since the first day of this month begins the whirlwind countdown to the year's end with all of its planning, shopping, and celebrating, be sure to include regular naps or at least daily peaceful escapes. Begin to slow the moments of today and change into your pajamas just as former presidents and geniuses always did for their quiet time.

In a comforting act of kindness, steep a single cup of African tea for yourself. Dissolve a teaspoon of raw sugar into the mahogany-colored beverage. Watch as the crystals swirl about and eventually disappear.

Invite the essence of chamomile to work its charm and refresh a batch of potpourri with six drops of this essential oil. Toss it lightly and display it in your designated nap corner. The essence's calming properties will sweep you into a satisfying daytime sleep. In extra softness reserved for a princess, lay a featherbed, a down comforter, or several comforters on the couch and settle on top.

Tuck a smaller fleece or flannel blanket around you and turn your attention to a few witty quotes. Read, laugh, and then nap. Afterward, revel in a few more moments of complete stillness before resuming your day in an unhurried manner.

> *The more faithfully you listen to the voice within you,*
> *the better you hear what is sounding outside of you.*
> —Dag (Hjalmar Agne Carl) Hammarskjöld (1905–1961)

DECEMBER: *Holiday Treat*

eggnog topped with whipped cream, nutmeg, and cardamom
goose down comforter
cedarwood room spray
Summer Nights **on a sound machine**
journal and pen

In the lands where the frozen ground hibernates six feet beneath a solid white blanket, faded tracks suggest that a small animal has not emerged from its den for days. When the clear air is still frosted mid afternoon, take a hint from Nature and burrow in for a long winter nap. Go in search of your warmest comforter, a few fluffy pillows, and fill the bed. Dust your winter haven in a refreshing room spray of cedarwood.

In the kitchen, warm up the day with a taste of the holiday season and pour yourself a mug of eggnog. Shower the velvety spiraling tower of whipped cream with a sprinkle of nutmeg and cardamom. On your nap tray, place your special holiday beverage, your journal, and a pen.

Climb into your comforter and pillow cave. Support your head and neck with one pillow, elevate your feet with another, and make a table out of a third. Prop up your journal and begin to write. Watch your worries fall onto the pages. Feel the stress in your shoulders lift and drift far away.

When you finish writing, turn on a sound machine or nature music. Close your eyes and imagine that you are entering a rain forest. The chorus of exotic parrots and frogs blends with the water music of a distant waterfall. From inside your winter home, dream of sun-filled days.

There's a certain slant of light, on winter afternoons…
—Emily Dickinson (1830–1886)

EXPECTATIONS
BY JOHN WILLIAM GODWARD

CHAPTER FIVE

Relaxation Techniques

MEDITATION, YOGA, AND MASSAGE

Life shrinks or expands in proportion to one's courage.
—*Anaïs Nin (1903–1977)*

People have sought paths to be at peace with themselves and the world since the dawn of time. All religions contain the recurring elements of meditation or prayer, yoga, and massage. Recently, many have turned to these ancient relaxation techniques to slow their fast-paced lives.

In all of the relaxation techniques suggested in this chapter, deep-breathing exercises are used. This conscious act of focusing on your breath can be a welcome escape, and equally beneficial, when a nap is not possible. There are two types of meditation: mindful meditation and moving meditation. Both can be employed to aid in relaxation.

Visualization or creative guided imagery can be employed to reduce worries and calm the spirit, allowing you to be completely enveloped in the peacefulness of each session.

Journaling is another positive way to put worries in perspective and work out possible solutions. Be sure to include affirmations in your journal or speak their positive statements aloud when in a relaxed state.

One of the best stress releasers, and available at no cost, is to spend an entire day outdoors, surrounded by nature. You can choose to be active and hike or bike, lounge in a hammock all afternoon, or read the day away in a park.

Yoga translates from Sanskrit to mean, "the union of the mind and body." With regular practice of postures and deep breathing, muscles are strengthened and toned, digestion, circulation, and balance are improved, fatigue and stress are abated, and the mind is cleared.

Massage, no longer veiled in mystery, is used to reduce heart rate, relax muscles, lessen pain, and produce a feeling of well-being through an increase in the production of endorphins. Give yourself the wonderful gift of massage and rid your body of tight spots where nervous tension resides.

These practices are also instrumental in keeping the mind and body youthful and vital. Choose a path with heart—one that you feel is right for you. The art of relaxation deserves to become a natural part in all of your days.

BREATHE DEEPLY

Breathing in and out through the nose calms the entire nervous system and connects the mind to the body. When you focus on this automatic reflex, you will achieve a moment of peace. Deep breathing can be done anywhere: in the shower, at a board meeting, or in a very long line at the post office. Try this: inhale to a count of four, exhale to a count of eight, repeat four times, and then smile.

During the 1950s, endocrinologist Dr. Hans Selye of Vienna, Austria-Hungary, identified that our emotional state affects our well-being when he studied the body's "fight or flight syndrome." He discovered that in a perceived threatening situation, our bodies automatically prepare to fight or to flee. We breathe through our mouths to increase the amount of oxygen to our bodies. Our blood pressure elevates, our heartbeat increases, and our muscles flex as we get ready for action. This inherited response from our ancestors is a result of their daily encounters with the natural environment, which included fierce animals or other warring tribes.

Today, as we deal with congested roadways, impossible deadlines, tricky technology, or other situations beyond our control, we become aggravated and the feeling never recedes. Our bodies react and remain in the fight or flight state. What we need in every day is the opposite reaction called the relaxation response.

Practice conscious breathing whenever tension fills your shoulders, the worry lines deepen on your forehead, or your head begins to pound. Try this: raise your eyebrows as high as you can and hold the stretch for the count of five. Repeat whenever you feel your face become tense.

Journaling

The act of putting your thoughts and emotions down on paper can help to cut through stress and eliminate worries. Pick up a pen and write away for twenty minutes. It does not matter if your spelling is bad or your sentences are incomplete. To get started journaling, write when you feel like it—every morning, every night, or every other day. Start on page one of a journal, the middle, or on the last page of a lined notebook with cartoons all over the cover to remind yourself that life should not be so serious.

Use the same pen—or not. Write every day—or not. There are no rules. This is your journal for you and you alone. If what you write makes you nervous, tear it up, toss it in the garbage, or burn it. However, a word to the wise: you may want to keep it to read later and learn how you managed your stress.

Journaling can take all types of forms. Sketches and doodles are allowed. New Year's resolutions are permitted in the middle of July. Letters to the source of your aggravation are definitely welcomed. Express how you feel. Write anything. After you are done getting it all out, take a couple of deep breaths, turn the page, and now write what you would do if you knew you would not fail.

Negative thoughts can affect how you feel, so always end your journaling on a positive note. Make a list of people who make you laugh, places you love to visit and dream of touring, or the colors you will someday paint your nap room. Draw a page of smiley faces if words escape you. Positive thoughts and words result in a positive attitude and positive actions. Be sure to end your journal entries in this happy frame of mind. It will make the rest of the day, or the next day, a brighter place to be.

AFFIRMATIONS

There is absolutely no doubt—your state of mind affects your health. Affirmations, or positive thoughts, are powerful medicine used by physicians, psychotherapists, coaches, motivational speakers, and religious leaders for decades.

Émile Coué, a French psychologist, is remembered for his formula to cure with optimistic autosuggestion: "Day by day, in every way, I am getting better and better." In the 1920s, his teaching brought the power of affirmations to the attention of the Western medical world. He had instructed his patients to focus on healing rather than the fear associated with illness and it worked.

Since the invention of the electroencephalogram (EEG) in the 1930s, scientists have been able to measure the brain's electrical activity and have determined the best time to program the mind by replacing negative thoughts with positive ones. During the quiet state of relaxation, when the alpha rhythms (our brain waves) are between eight and thirteen cycles per second, is considered the optimal time to positively influence the mind. Affirmations are able to pass through our internal gatekeeper, the left hemisphere, responsible for self-doubt, guilt, and nay-saying because this critical censoring center is half asleep.

In your journal writings and conversations with yourself, be sure to include affirmations to improve your life one day at a time. Express your affirmations in your own words. Be positive and use the present tense. By committing your convictions to paper, you are taking one step closer to achieving your goal. Say them aloud three times a day—when you awaken in the morning, during meditation, and before you go to sleep.

Try any of these affirmations this week:

I give myself permission to nap.

I will be patient with my body during yoga.

I will be kind to myself.

ELEMENTS OF NATURE

Nature is a wonderful place to seek peace and tranquillity, even in such human-enhanced form as an Elizabethan maze, a Japanese rock garden, or a sculpture garden. Going outside is one of the best stress-reduction remedies. Nature always has a soothing effect on the spirit, whether we are actively engaged, such as walking or white-water rafting, or passively observing, sitting quietly under a tree or on a rock by a stream.

Discover the environment outdoors and find peace. Truly be in nature: ski down a black diamond and know inner strength. Climb up the same slope on a mountain bike come August and understand the depth of endurance. Raft the white waters and feel a new sense of confidence. Fish a quiet pond or hike to the top of a mountain and camp alone. When you explore nature, you will be discovering yourself.

We all need nature in our lives every day, yet we forget it is everywhere. In a city, there is a park, a flower shop, or a garden café. We can bring the outdoors inside and fill our homes with real plants. Water them weekly and they will purify the air you breathe daily. We breathe out carbon dioxide. They breathe it in and say, "Thank you" with a big exhalation of oxygen. Take plants to the office and your workspace instantly becomes more attractive and healthier. It is an easy and mutually beneficial relationship.

MEDITATION

Your vision will become clear only when you look into your heart...who looks outside,
dreams, who looks inside, awakens.

—Carl Jung (1875–1961)

Recent studies at Harvard Medical School used magnetic resonating imagery (MRI) technology to monitor brain activity while participants meditated. The findings showed that meditation could activate sections of the brain that we cannot normally control, including the nervous, digestive, and circulatory systems. Researchers concluded that if we modulate these functions, we can ward off potential problems caused by stress, such as heart disease, digestive troubles, and infertility.

The American Heart Association asserts that those who meditate daily can reduce their risks of heart attack and stroke. Statistics from health insurance companies report that people who meditate regularly are less prone to illness and reduce their chances of being hospitalized for coronary disease by 87 percent and of getting cancer by 55 percent.

Daily meditation practice relieves stress, promotes healing, and helps you experience a deeper level of composure, integrity, and clarity in your busy days. When meditating, the body moves into the same state as when you are asleep. Oxygen consumption, heart and breathing rates, and the activity in the brain-wave patterns are reduced. These changes experienced are not subjective, but measurable—brain-wave frequencies decrease from thirteen to thirty cycles per second to eight to thirteen cycles per second. The brain increases its production of endorphins, the proteins in the body responsible for making us feel good. As many people are beginning to discover, meditation benefits the entire person: physically, mentally, emotionally, and spiritually.

Seven Components of Meditation

Quiet and safe environment free of loud noises or distractions
Comfortable position and loose, comfortable clothing
Dedicated time, from five minutes to twenty, preferably at the same time every day
Focusing method that works for you
Deep breathing, inhaling and exhaling through the nose
Uncritical or nonjudgmental attitude
Gradual and unhurried return to regular activities afterward

YOGA

Namasté. *(The light in me honors the light in you.)*
—*greeting in yoga class*

Yoga, the five thousand–year-old Indian practice, is growing in popularity because it is ageless and its benefits are felt inside as well as seen on the outside. Regular practice relieves a variety of stress-related diseases including hypertension, heart problems, and ulcers. The *asanas*, or poses, in yoga flex and stretch the spine and exercise joints and muscles. Yoga also stimulates all the systems: circulation, nervous, digestive, and endocrine to keep you healthy in body as well as mind and spirit.

Yoga does not require a lot of equipment or expense. For class or your private session with a video, simply wear loose clothing. You may want a long-sleeved shirt or sweatshirt over a tank top or T-shirt so you can remove a layer when you are warmed up and put it back on for the cool-down phases of the session. No shoes or socks are required—just come in bare feet. You might want to use a towel to cushion your knees when kneeling, a yoga strap for some stretches, or blocks for balance. Eventually, you will want to purchase your own mat to bring with you to class or for practice at home. Many instructors and students prefer the solid-colored, thin, sticky mats to aid with balance. Others choose the two-inch thick fabric mats filled with untreated cotton (36" x 70").

There are many different schools of yoga, ranging from slow and meditative Hatha yoga to a vigorous workout such as Ashtanga yoga, or power yoga. Try them all—you will find the method that suits you best. You may want a slow practice some days and a more strenuous one on others.

Class starts by sitting quietly and focusing on your breath. Meditative music may play softly. As the yoga instructor moves you into the second, or warm-up, phase, you will feel the heat in your muscles. The class will end in a resting pose called the corpse pose or *savasana*.

In yoga, there is no judgment, no competition. No matter where you are in a pose—that is exactly where you are supposed to be. Yoga is a continuous mind-body journey that will affect you differently every session. At home, play low spiritual or New Age music in the background to heighten this time. Set time aside regularly for yoga. Ask all thoughts to leave your mind and let stress melt into the floor. Be there for you and only you.

YOGA PRACTICE

Once you have attended several classes or have referenced a picture book from the library, you may want to set up your own yoga routine.

To begin, always warm up the body and mind with a series of deep-breathing exercises. Breathe through your nose to regulate speed and depth. Experiment with various exercises: count your breath, focus on filling your lungs, or breathe oxygen into all the far corners of your body. If you ever feel pain while doing a yoga posture, come out of the pose and relax in a resting pose such as the Corpse, Child's Pose, or Downward Facing Dog Pose.

When you are ready, slowly enter the pose again, but only to the point of maximum sensation. During some of the poses, you may want to close your eyes to limit visual distractions. In other poses, closing your eyes will challenge your balance. You may opt to soften your focus and look at a spot on the floor or wall to keep extraneous thoughts and visual stimuli to a minimum. Mentally picture each pose as a three-step process: entering, holding, and exiting. Do not rush. Move at your own pace. Be gentle with yourself and listen to your body.

You can also enjoy yoga with your children. Because they are naturally flexible, children love moving in and out of the poses and many positions have animals names that make the postures extra fun. Children may bark in Downward Dog or hiss in Cobra. Remember to warm up the bodies of the little students with deep, dragon-fire breathing through the nose and slow stretches to the sky, ground, and out toward their neighbors before launching into the poses. Avoid the use of inverted postures with children so as not to affect their glandular systems. There are many good yoga tapes and books for children. Check your local health food store or the pages of *Yoga Journal*.

Yoga is wonderful for expectant mothers and provides the exercise the changing body craves and needs. Always consult with your doctor first before starting any exercise program. If during the third trimester you feel a shift in your center of gravity, use a chair, the wall, or blocks to help with any yoga pose. *Caution: Pregnant women are advised to avoid lying on their backs and on their left sides and not to do lower spinal twists and inversions. Always check with a trained practitioner and listen to your body.*

SOME BASIC YOGA POSTURES

Instead of the usual cup of coffee or tea this morning, try yoga. Start your early yoga session with a warm bath or shower, but let your body return to its normal temperature before starting your practice. A brisk fifteen-minute walk will warm up the body from the inside and is another good way to focus on one new pose or to try a few. If you sit all day at the office, consider a yoga break to do a few standing postures or sitting postures right in your chair. Even five minutes of deep breathing and stretches will refresh and energize you.

Mountain Pose—Stand with your feet hip-distance apart and the outside of your feet parallel. To find your balance, rock back and forth from your tiptoes back to your heels. Do this several times to locate your balance. Come to a centered stance and close your eyes.

Gently let your shoulder blades slide down to a relaxed position. Feel the top of your head reach toward the ceiling to further elongate your spine. Keep your knees straight, but not locked. Let your palms face forward by your side, away from your body at a comfortable angle and distance.

Feel connected to the Earth through your feet. Listen to your body breathe. Open your eyes and exhale a breath of thanks to your body for carrying you every day. This is an important balancing pose from which many other yoga poses start.

Seated Twist—Sit up straight on the ground with your right leg straight. Pull your left leg tight into your chest, placing your left foot firmly on the floor. Hug your left knee close to you, with your right arm snugly around the shin. Inhale and twist your head and body to look over your left shoulder. Place your other hand on the floor behind you at a comfortable distance away from your body. Keep your back straight. When you are ready, untwist and switch legs. Repeat this pose equally on both sides several times.

If sitting in a chair, keep your right foot on the ground and pull your left leg up on to the chair and hug it with your right arm. Twist your upper body and look over your left shoulder. Push energy down through your right heel. Hold the Seated Twist Pose and take several deep breaths. Untwist and switch sides. Repeat the pose equally on both sides several times.

Cat/Cow Stretch—Kneel on all fours and spread your fingertips wide with your thumbs pointing toward one another. Equally distribute your weight on your fingers, palms, and wrists, as well as on your knees and feet. Place your hands beneath your shoulders and align your knees directly under your hips. If discomfort occurs, place a folded towel under your knees.

To begin the Cat Stretch Pose, inhale and round your back. Look at your belly button and allow your head to hang. To move into the Cow Stretch Pose, exhale, drop your stomach toward the floor, and look up toward the distant horizon. Your chin, chest, and tailbone should turn upward in this pose.

At your own pace, continue to work your breath with each stretch, holding before releasing into the next pose. This is a flowing pose used to stretch the spine. Feel free to reverse the breathing on this pose if it feels more natural.

MASSAGE

Learn to feel joy.

—*Seneca (4 B.C.–A.D.65)*

Massage relaxes muscle tension, alleviates stress, relieves pain, and most importantly, can help you get the sleep your body needs. Massage is also beneficial for those who exercise regularly because it increases the supply of blood to the muscles, flushes lactic acid and other metabolic waste, relaxes spasms, maintains joint mobility, and helps prevent cramps, stiffness, and injuries.

Massage aficionados hold the belief that we are composed of much more than just organs, muscles, and bones. For thousands of years, many cultures have acknowledged that there is life force, or energy, within all of us. In Japan, it is called *ki*, in China, *chi*, and in India, *prana*. In the early 1980s, Dr. Kim Bong-han, a Korean medical professor, showed that the electrical current of our bodies could be traced along the meridians illustrated in ancient texts. Massage is one relaxation technique used to correct energy flow and renew the spirit.

HAND SHIATSU

Shiatsu is a style of massage that applies pressure to the body with the fingertips to deal with the underlying energy balance and to improve overall vitality. If you engage in repetitive tasks such as typing, a sixty-second hand shiatsu is a very beneficial massage. Quick and simple, it is the perfect "at-work" massage because it is an instant mood changer. Dot the center of your palm with massage oil and rub your hands together to distribute the oil. Take care not to take too much, otherwise it is difficult to hold onto your fingers. With the thumb and forefinger of your left hand, start at the edge of your right wrist closest to your little finger. Gently and slowly squeeze from the palm to the end of your little finger. Use friction on each knuckle.

Tightly hold the finger pad for a few seconds. Return to the base of your wrist and continue on all fingers. Next, hold your right hand in the palm of the left. Use the left thumb to stroke the right palm in a circular motion. Start small and gradually enlarge the circle until the entire palm has been massaged.

Repeat this massage on your left hand. To end the session, rub your palms together. When they begin to heat up, shake your hands in front of you and roll your wrists in a circular motion a few times in each direction.

FOOT SHIATSU

Pampering Foot Massage

2 tbsp. sunflower carrier oil

2 tbsp. sweet almond carrier oil

4 drops sandalwood essential oil

2 drops clary sage essential oil

2 drops jasmine essential oil

Since your feet deserve attention, treat them kindly and your whole body will feel good, too. To enjoy this massage, sit somewhere quiet, place your right foot on your thigh, and let it extend over your leg. Pour a nickel-size amount of massage oil out on your hands and rub them together. Start below the toes and massage the sole in small circular motions. Move to the center and then to the heel. With your thumb, make circular motions on the inner side of the heel several times and then gently squeeze the tendon at the back of the ankle. On the inner side of the foot, lightly walk your thumb from your ankle toward your big toe.

Between each toe, use your thumb and index finger to press down on the tendons. Next, with your forefinger and thumb, start at the big toe and squeeze from the base of each toe to the pad. End with a squeeze at the tip. Wrap your foot in a towel, add more oil to your hands, and massage your other foot. When you finish the massage, wrap both feet in the towel and relax for five minutes longer.

Shoulders and Neck Massage

Goodbye Stress Massage

4 tbsp. grapeseed carrier oil

1 tbsp. jojoba carrier oil

4 drops lavender essential oil

3 drops neroli essential oil

2 drops chamomile essential oil

Ideal for sending stress away at the end of a busy afternoon, use this blend to give yourself a shoulders and neck massage. Your partner will probably agree to give you this wonderful massage if you promise to return the favor. If necessary, pull up long hair and remove earrings. Afterward, wrap up in a bathrobe for a while and rest.

Leg Massage

Beautiful Legs Treatment

4 tbsp. peach kernel carrier oil

5 drops frankincense essential oil

3 drops clary sage essential oil

This soothing massage will help achy legs and rejuvenate your entire system. Arrange some pillows to support your back and elevate your legs before you begin. Cover the pillows with towels so not to get oil on the pillowcases. When massaging, do not break the contact between your hands and skin. Turn your hand over, palm up against the skin, to replenish the oil. Bend your knee. Use broad strokes on the thigh. Cover the knee area, front and back, with a gentle motion.

Reach to the ankle and slowly pull on the muscles toward your knee. Repeat, sliding back down to the ankle and back to the knee again. Spend time massaging the calf muscles and end with a pulling motion from the ankle the entire way up your leg to the top of your thigh. Repeat this massage on your other leg after reapplying oils to your palms.

MUSCULAR MASSAGE

Sore Body Massage

4 tbsp. sweet almond carrier oil

6 drops lavender essential oil

5 drops peppermint essential oil

4 drops eucalyptus essential oil

Treat your sore muscles to this delightful massage. Pour the oils into shallow bowl or flip-top bottle and mix them well. Massage all the sore areas of your body. Cover yourself with a warm towel or wrap up in a robe and settle back for a well-deserved break.

Pregnancy Massage

Babying the New Mom-to-Be

4 tbsp. sweet almond carrier oil

3 drops rose essential oil

2 drops neroli essential oil

Expectant mothers deserve all the attention they can get before the baby arrives. In the first four months, sit with your feet elevated for a very gentle massage over the abdomen. After the fifth month, it is best to lie on your right side for a light, comforting massage. For a neck and shoulder massage, sit or recline with pillows supporting your back and arms. For a leg massage, you might have to enlist someone else's help! Raise your knees with pillows so that your feet dangle and your partner can massage your lower legs and feet.

Geranium, lemon, neroli, orange, rose, and sandalwood are considered safe for mother and baby, but check with your doctor first or with a trained aromatherapist. If you have had a history of miscarriage, avoid chamomile and lavender for the first few months—although in general, these oils are excellent for your pregnancy in later months.

Due to their strong diuretic properties or tendency to induce menstruation, avoid bay, basil, clary sage, comfrey, fennel, hyssop, juniper, marjoram, Melissa, myrrh, rosemary, thyme, and sage. Also, because of their potentially toxic nature and strong abortive qualities, avoid oreganum, pennyroyal, St. John's Wort, tansy, and wormwood.

As you move closer to motherhood, enjoy and cherish this special time. Start a healthy ritual of massage for yourself along with a nap so it will be easy to maintain this habit once the little one joins your household.

PEACE ROSE
BY K.S. ROBISCHON

CHAPTER SIX

Enter an Enlightened World

AROMATHERAPY

Make the most of every sense; glory in all the pleasures
and beauty which the world reveals to you.
—Helen Keller (1880–1968)

Welcome to the gentle world of aromatherapy. Few luxuries in this life are as simple and as pleasing. Essential oils can be used to create a mood and encourage a most wondrous feeling of well-being. And essential oils do influence the psyche, directly affecting mood and emotion and causing a response in the central nervous system and brain.

French chemist Dr. René-Maurice Gattefossé named the therapy that used essential oils *aromathérapie* in 1928. Scientists from many different disciplines—biochemistry, biology, chemistry, medicine, psychiatry, sociology, as well as the perfume industry—all acknowledge the significant importance of smell and its therapeutic benefits.

From the approximately two hundred essential oils commercially extracted from pure plants, the following thirteen essences are recommended to relieve stress and fatigue and assist with relaxation.

CEDARWOOD

Cedrus Atlantica / Juniperus Virginiana

dry, woodsy, strong, balsam-like essence with an exhilarating scent

warming, comforting, strengthening

The wood for a temple does not come from a single tree.

—*Chinese proverb*

Frequently mentioned in the Bible, the majestic cedar, which can grow more than one hundred feet in height, is known throughout the world as "the tree of life" or "the tree of gods." If a cedar tree is left to nature without any interference, it can reach an age of one thousand to two thousand years. Recognized as a symbol of faith and strength, it is no coincidence that its Latin root means "strong."

Revered for its relaxing and meditative properties, cedarwood is one of the oldest essential oils. Noted at the start of recorded history, the Egyptians included cedarwood as an important ingredient in cosmetics, perfumes, and medicine, and in their mummification rituals. Cleopatra, a true believer in the powers of aromatherapy, ringed her throne with incense burners to diffuse various essences of oils into the air. She allegedly received Antony on a barge made of cedarwood. During the nineteenth century, Europeans added the essence of cedarwood to cold creams and soaps and splashed handkerchiefs with the oil.

For therapeutic use, insist on the bottles labeled *cedrus altantica*. This is the true cedar distilled from the Atlas Cedars growing in the Atlas Mountains of Morocco. Cedarwood oil has been prescribed to promote restful sleep, open the sinus and breathing passages, ease chest congestion, improve mental clarity, and relieve anxiety and nervous tension. Other bottled essences of cedarwood, *juniperus virginiana* or *juniperus mexicana*, are actually fragrant oil distilled from red cedar trees grown in North America. This oil is not for the body.

Applications:
❦ *blends well with clary sage, jasmine, lavender, neroli, rose, sandalwood, and ylang ylang*
❦ *mixes easily with most carrier oils*
❦ *repels moths*
Caution: Avoid during pregnancy.

CLARY SAGE

Salvia Sclarea

strong, spicy, herbal fragrance with a wine-like nuance and intriguing musk undertones

relaxing, warming, balancing

I dwell in possibility…

—Emily Dickinson (1830–1886)

Ancient lore tells of white-magic spells made with clary sage. Believers claim that the essence is instrumental in igniting the interest of a desired love. Be careful of who enters the room as this magical essence is being released.

For aromatherapy and therapeutic use, select the essential oil bottled as *salvia sclarea*. Common sage is called *salvia officinalis*. Watch for the different labels when purchasing.

Clary sage uplifts the spirit, warms the soul, and relaxes the body. It has been used to aid with digestion, to relieve stress and tension, and to promote a restful sleep. With a scent similar to lavender, this lovely but powerful essence is likened to a good bottle of champagne, and is known to produce a feeling of mild intoxication and encourage creativity—without a hangover. Add this essence to your haven for inspiration when you write in your journal, paint, garden, or sew.

Applications:

❦ *blends well with lavender, geranium, patchouli, and rose*
❦ *mixes well with grapeseed oil*

Caution: Due to the relaxing effect of this oil, do not use it before driving or any task that requires your full attention.

In large amounts, clary sage can be stupefying.

Perfumed Clary Sage Handkerchief

To aid in falling asleep at naptime, lightly dab a handkerchief with two or three drops of clary sage. Sniff the essence from a bit of a distance. Essential oils are very powerful and a little goes a long way. Tuck it away in your desk or lingerie drawer to enjoy the scent again the next time you open it.

EUCALYPTUS

Eucalyptus Globulus

fresh, slightly balsamic with an agreeable, woodsy, sweet aroma

purifying, releasing, refreshing

...who plants a tree, plants a hope.

—Lucy Larcom (1824–1893)

In their homeland of Australia, eucalyptus trees are known commonly as gum trees. Their bark exudes the sweet-smelling resin, yet it is the silvery, blue-green leaves of the mature trees that contain the droplets of essential oil and yield a better aromatic quality than younger saplings. The eucalyptus tree can grow seventy to ninety feet in two short decades, with the tallest of these nonconifers reaching between three hundred to four hundred and eighty feet.

Over the centuries, many have relied on the essence for its anti-inflammatory, antiseptic, and antibacterial properties and recognize eucalyptus as the active ingredient in cough drops and syrups. When the essence is used as a room spray, a pleasing aroma blankets the area while killing germs. Add it to a facial sauna or a diffuser and the aromatic essence will help fight sore throats. This winter season, keep away colds by lightly misting the bed linens. Eucalyptus is also an ideal essential oil to use for massage because it evaporates quickly.

When used in aromatherapy, eucalyptus is key to a sound nap. This soothing essence encourages the body temperature to cool and makes napping easy.

Applications:
❦ *blends well with cedarwood and lavender*
❦ *insect repellant*

Koala Steam Shower

As you prepare for your day's respite, run a very hot shower and capture the steam in the bathroom. Close the door, block the crack at the bottom with a towel, and do not run the fan. Fill a spray bottle with warm water and five drops of eucalyptus. Shake well. Turn on the shower and enter. Spray the area around you, avoiding your face and eyes. Breathe in the refreshing aroma. Close your eyes and pretend you are in a forest of eucalyptus trees.

FRANKINCENSE

Boswellia Thurifera / Boswellia Carteri
rich, woodsy, earthy scent, subtly lemony with a note of pepper
clearing, visualizing, restorative

Holy Mother Earth, the trees and all nature are witnesses of your thoughts and deeds.
—*North American Winnebago Indian saying*

Frankincense means "luxuriant incense" and is mentioned in the Bible twenty-two times. The essential oil is distilled from the aromatic gum of the leafy tree, *boswellia thurifera*, which grows in North Africa and the Middle East. This small tree, reaching a height of ten to twenty feet, is related to the myrrh-producing tree. Used by aromatherapists today, frankincense can effectively treat respiratory complaints and calm the spirit. Like cedarwood, frankincense draws the body and mind into the here and now.

Applications:
❦ *blends well with geranium, lavender, neroli, and sandalwood*

Perfume

Aromatic Jewel Perfume

1 tbsp. jojoba carrier oil

2 tbsp. sunflower carrier oil

7 drops frankincense essential oil

6 drops rosewood essential oil

1 drop ylang ylang essential oil

Feel like a queen for the day and wear this designer perfume. Gently swirl the essential oils and jojoba oil together. Dot this exotic blend on the inside of your wrists, ankles, or at the base of your neck. Store your signature fragrance in a dark glass bottle for future enjoyment. Sink into a pile of pillows and sleep, dreaming of being waited on hand and foot.

Fragrant Firewood

Make any wintry afternoon instantly warmer with this grounding, earthy scent. Splash five drops of frankincense onto a few firewood logs and wait until the oil dries. Start a fire in the fireplace and sit back to benefit from the aroma.

GERANIUM

Geranium Maculatum / Pelargonium Graveolens / Pelargoium Odoratissimum
delightfully refreshing with a rosy, lemon, orange, apple, nutmeg, or chocolate fragrance
sustaining, restoring, balancing

Every flower is a soul blossoming in nature.
—*Gérard de Nerval (1805–1855)*

The French word *potpourri* means "rot pot." Original recipes were made of moist mixtures, not like the contemporary dried concoctions now used in linen sachets and pillows and displayed in decorative containers.

Sweet geraniums with their mimicry of scents are easy to grow. The seventy-five scented varieties available include the floral fragrance of rose, the fruit aromas of strawberry, apple, apricot, lime, and coconut, as well as hints of spices such as chocolate, nutmeg, pepper, eucalyptus, filbert, peppermint, almond, and also the pungent aroma of pine. Since the volatile oils are released by a touch to the foliage, the next time you visit a nursery, gently rub a leaf of a scented geranium between your fingers and then sniff to identify its aroma.

Today, more than seven hundred species are grown simply for their charm, yet some are cultivated for essential oils. The essence of geranium is also sometimes sold as Geranium Bourbon-la-Reunion, named after the French island, Reunion, in the Indian Ocean where this plant is cultivated.

The sweet aroma of geranium brings a sense of equilibrium and allows the body to be in perfect harmony with the mind and spirit. Traditionally, its essential oil has been used to treat skin, circulatory, reproductive, and respiratory disorders. Effective as an antidepressant, essence of geranium is an excellent relaxant for those suffering from nervous tension.

There are many ways to enjoy scented geraniums or the plant's essential oil: float a sprig of lemon-scented geranium in a finger bowl for guests or release the essence of geranium via a diffuser to harmonize a new mother's emotions. Invite the sensation of summer to linger all year long and bring a potted plant indoors. With blooming geraniums placed inside the foyer, centered on the dining room table, or in a corner of your nap sanctuary, you and your home will be naturally refreshed.

Applications:

❦ *mixes well with lavender, jasmine, rose, neroli, patchouli, and sandalwood*

❦ *repels mosquitoes*

Caution: Avoid essential oil of geranium in the first three months of pregnancy.

Soothing Room Fragrance

Many retailers offer mixtures conveniently packaged, but neither aerosols nor artificial ingredients are good for the environment or for your health. Instead, mix your own room fragrance. Simply add twelve drops of geranium oil to a dark glass spray bottle and fill it with water. Shake well and perfume the room, pillows, linens, and couch with your personal mix. Choose a light-colored essential oil and test spray an inconspicuous area first to make sure the oil does not mark your fabrics.

Release the wonderful summer aroma of geranium with a light spritz of your new room spray. Breathe deeply and feel your spirits lift instantly.

Potpourri

Country Garden Potpourri

1 cup dried lemon-scented geranium flowers

1 cup dried lemon-scented geranium leaves

1 cup dried lavender flowers

1 cup dried rose petals

1 cup dried hydrangea flowers

2 tsp. allspice

1 tbsp. ground cinnamon

1 tsp. dried lemon peel

2 tbsp. orrisroot powder

15 drops geranium essential oil

15 drops rose essential oil

Gently toss the flowers and leaves with the spices. Add the lemon peel. Combine the orrisroot powder with the essential oils. Stir well, but lightly. Store your potpourri in a covered container in a dark, dry place. Every other day, gently move the potpourri from one container to another to distribute the fragrance and avoid damaging the fragile elements. In about a month, your fragrant and decorative mix will be ready.

Jasmine

Jasminum Offinale / Jasmine Officinalis / Jasminium Grandiflorum
rich, fruity fragrance with a honey-like sweetness
balancing, calming, warming

Perfumes rarely come from the flowers whose names they bear,
except jasmine, which is impossible to counterfeit.
—Joris-Karl Huysmans (1848–1907)

In Asia, the land where this delicate, star-shaped white blossom originated, jasmine is regarded as a sacred flower. A hardy and deciduous evergreen climbing shrub with white and pink-tinted flowers, it is called "the king of flowers."

For centuries, the exotic scent of jasmine represented the emblem for love and was included as a key ingredient in spells and potions. Considered an aphrodisiac for women, jasmine is believed to make the mind more receptive to feelings of love and compassion.

The most fragrant jasmine flowers bloom from August to September and exude an exquisite aroma mostly at night. Jasmine must be handpicked after the sun has set to gain the full therapeutic value in application as an essential oil. One of the most expensive oils in the world, very little of this essential oil is needed due to its intense scent. No synthetic blend has yet been found to replicate the lavish aroma of natural jasmine. This essence, prescribed to aid with skincare problems, abate pain, depression, and breathing difficulties, is so exquisite and powerful that many claim that merely smelling its fragrance can lift spirits.

Applications:

❦ mixes well with clary sage, rose, and sandalwood
If you find jasmine too expensive, try ylang ylang for an equally exotic aroma.

Scented Jasmine Linen Paper

Add the wondrous fragrance of jasmine to your dresser drawers. Select parchment paper, shelf paper, or attractive wallpaper. Cut the paper to fit the inside of your drawers or to line your closet shelves. Layer dried jasmine flowers between the sheets with the adhesive side, or nondecorative side, touching the flowers. Next, dot four cotton balls with a few drops of jasmine oil and place them between the sheets alongside the blossoms. Slide the stacked sheets with the flowers and cotton balls in place into plastic bags and seal them. Store them flat in a dark, dry location.

After two weeks, the paper will absorb the perfume of the flowers and essence. Before placing the scented paper, dot the inside of the drawers with fresh cotton balls dabbed in the essential oil of jasmine.

Scented Laundry

Fragrant Laundry Rinse Water

3 cups of jasmine flowers

2 quarts of water

Place the flowers in a saucepan and cover them with water. Bring the water to a boil. Cover the pan and remove it from the heat. Allow the water to cool to lukewarm, strain the flowers from the water, and capture them in a decorative bottle or jar. Seal it tightly. Store the laundry rinse water in a cool, dry place or refrigerate it. Pour ¼ cup into the washer during the rinse cycle for scented fresh towels, linens, and clothing.

LAVENDER

Lavandula Angustifolia / Lavandula Officinalis

clean, fresh, floral aroma with a woodsy undertone

clarifying, soothing, restoring

Art is the unceasing effort to compete with the beauty of flowers—and never succeeding.
—Marc Chagall (1887–1985)

This fragrant, evergreen shrub is native to southern Europe, particularly in the Mediterranean. The aroma of lavender relaxes the body and balances the moods, creating a sense of timelessness. If you are agitated, the essence is calming. If you are lethargic, the fragrance is stimulating. Check to see if your selection is true lavender labeled *lavandula officinalis* or *lavandula angustifolia*, the English Lavender.

To enjoy this popular and versatile plant, hang wands of lavender tied together with twine upside down from a nail or rafter. When the flowers are dried, weave the stems together to form a handle and tie it with a ribbon. Place the dried lavender bunch in linen drawers as an effective way to repel moths. Lavender is heavenly when milled in soaps and scented candles. It is also delicious in tea, cheese, and bread.

Applications:

❦ *blends well with clary sage, cedarwood, geranium, and patchouli*
❦ *burn incense as a natural bug repellent*
❦ *mix essential oil with furniture polish to give oak a high gloss*

Caution: While lavender is the least toxic of essential oils, care should still be taken if you are pregnant. Check with your doctor first. You may be advised to avoid the essential oil of lavender during the first three months of pregnancy.

Insect Guard

In your linen and clothing closets, add cotton balls dabbed with the essential oil of lavender to deter moths and other pesky bugs, including silverfish, fleas, and flies.

Refreshment

Lavender Lemonade

4 tbsp. lavender buds

1 cup boiling water

1 frozen can of lemonade

spring or sparkling water

Boil the water. Pour one cup of boiling water over four tablespoons of lavender buds. Steep for ten minutes, then strain the buds from the liquid. Make frozen lemonade with the lavender infusion and spring or sparkling water. Chill it and serve it in a tall glass. Add ice cubes with a raspberry frozen in the center or garnish the glass with lemon balm, lemon verbena leaves, or a lemon twist.

NEROLI

Citrus Aurantium / Citrus Bigaradia

heavy, floral aroma with a sweet, orange undertone

calming, soothing, strengthening

When eating fruit, think of the person who planted the tree.

——*Vietnamese proverb*

Neroli oil is distilled from the white flowers of the bitter orange tree, *citrus autrantium*, or the Seville orange tree, *citrus bigaradia*, which favors the Mediterranean or subtropical climates. A native of Asia, these trees can grow to be thirty feet tall and produce up to sixty pounds of fresh flowers. This fragrant orange tree produces three essential oils: neroli, the most exquisite, orange, used to ease stress, and petitgrain, to banish fatigue and jet lag. Neroli is quite expensive with two tons of flowers required to produce only two pounds of the essential oil.

Used to treat stress-related illnesses, insomnia, and nervous tension, it is believed that the properties of neroli possess a very positive, calming influence on the mind and body. This essential oil acts like a natural tranquilizer and is an ideal selection to use before yoga or meditation. The essence of neroli's relaxing and enthralling scent is a welcome relief from a busy day at the office or a full day at home with children.

Applications:
❧ *mixes well with virtually all essential oils*
❧ *combine with rose or jasmine for a* crème de la crème *aromatherapy experience*

Sweet Orange Padded Hangers

As a gift to a new homeowner or for yourself, dab six dots of neroli essence on the bottom of decorative, padded hangers. Wrap them in tissue paper and tie them with a ribbon.

PATCHOULI

Pogostemon Patchouli / Cablin Patchouli

deep, earthy aroma with a musky, sensual scent

sedative, calming, warming

All things are artificial, for nature is the art of God.
—*Thomas Browne (1605–1682)*

This powerful essence has always played a large part in Asian medicines. It is considered effective against fevers, epidemics, and other illnesses. Its beneficial properties have aided with symptoms of depression, inflammation, and indigestion. When this essence is used in small amounts, it can be a stimulant, however, it becomes a sedative in large doses.

Patchouli can be adulterated with cubeb and cedar oils, so carefully read the labels. While synthetic patchouli has been produced, it has not met with much commercial success. It is now generally agreed by the industry that it is nearly impossible to replicate the lasting scent of patchouli. When the first whiff of this exotic, rich scent touches your olfactory senses, it will forever be fixed in your memory. Patchouli is one of the very few oils—this essence like fine wine—that improves with age.

Choose this essence when your nerves are irritated. This essential oil calms anxiety with its strong, earthy scent and can be most appropriate after a long day.

Applications:
☙ *mixes well with cedarwood, frankincense, geranium, jasmine, lavender,*
☙ *neroli, rose, sandalwood, and ylang ylang*
☙ *repels moths, fleas, and lice*
If patchouli is too overpowering, substitute sandalwood.

Fragrant Inks
Add five drops of patchouli to brown or violet ink and write only correspondence of good news.

Scented Stones
Buy or create your own box of nature. This small package of aromatherapy is easy to make. Lightly mist smooth river pebbles with the essence of patchouli. Package the scented rocks in a wooden box

to transport this intoxicating and settling earthy scent with you any day. When the workday has become too long, slide the lid open and be reminded of nature.

ROSE

Rosa Damascena / Rosa Centifolia / Rosa Gallica

copiously fragrant with an exquisite cherry-like perfume

balancing, soothing, sedative

She looks as clear as morning roses newly washed with dew.
—William Shakespeare (1564–1616)

The rose is the most celebrated flower in history. The rose has forever had a natural affinity with the heart, as it is the symbol of Venus, the Roman goddess of love. The custom of presenting a bouquet of red roses to proclaim passion and love for the lucky recipient began in the early Victorian days, a tradition that still continues today.

The most prized oil, otto of rose, also called rose attar, comes from the Damask rose, *Rose damascena*, cultivated in Bulgaria. To capture the flower's therapeutic and fragrant properties at their peak, the bud of the rose blossom must be handpicked just after the early morning dew. Unfortunately, this small window of time yields so little oil because thirty Damask roses are required to make one drop of this expensive essential oil.

For therapeutic use, select otto of rose or rose attar because this oil has been extracted by steam or distilled without heat or chemicals. Absolute oil, which has been produced by the use of a solvent, is less pure than attar.

The adage, "Take the time to stop and smell the roses," could be the best advice for those who live in a frantic, nonstop world. Rose possesses a potent, antidepressant effect and has been used to treat nervousness, sadness, and long-term stress. When released through a diffuser, the essence balances an unsettled system. Today, decide to include roses in your day. Float a handful of rose petals on bath water for its aromatic and visual appeal. Color a garden salad with a few edible petals or stir some into raspberry iced tea.

Applications:
❧ *blends well with clary sage, geranium, jasmine, lavender, patchouli, and sandalwood*
❧ *Rose Absolute is an economical alternative to rose otto.*
Caution: During the first four months of pregnancy, avoid using essential oil of rose.

Facial Sauna

Royal Rose Facial Sauna

2 quarts of boiling water

5 drops of rose essential oil

3 rose petals

Treat yourself like royalty and take time before your nap for this lovely treat. Wrap your hair in towel or pull it away from your face. Gently wash and pat dry your face. Pour boiling water into a ceramic bowl and add rose essential oil. Stir and add a few rose petals. With another towel, create a tent over the steaming bowl and enjoy this fragrant treatment for five minutes.

Scented Stationery

Add five drops of rose essential oil to a dark glass spray bottle filled with water. Mist several sheets of stationery and let them dry overnight. Send only messages from the heart on your new paper.

SANDALWOOD

Santalum Album

rich, velvety, woodsy aroma with a warm, fruit-like fragrance

warming, softening, soothing

I think that I shall never see a poem lovely as a tree.

—Joyce Kilmer (1886–1918)

Today, everything in the district of Mysore, India, the heart of the plantations, smells of sandalwood. When the tree is between forty and fifty years old, it is felled because this is when the tree has the greatest oil content. These evergreen trees with small purple flowers and fruit are native to southern Asia, but they are also found in the Pacific Islands and Australia.

The sumptuous aroma of sandalwood counteracts negative feelings and provides a relaxing and supportive environment ideal for meditation. Its essence enhances the peace of mind that occurs during sittings. Sandalwood is also a good choice for a massage because its oil evaporates slowly, so its therapeutic properties can effectively soothe a tired body.

Applications:

❦ *blends well with chamomile, geranium, lavender, jasmine, patchouli, and rose*
Caution: Watch for purity because sandalwood can be adulterated
with castor, palm, and linseed oils.

Scented Linens

For a peaceful sleep and to keep the linens smelling wonderful, dot several cotton balls with the essential oil of sandalwood and tuck them in your linen closet or chest.

YLANG YLANG

Cananga Odorata
extraordinary fragrance with high notes of hyacinth and narcissus
calming, relaxing, balancing

The way to health is to have an aromatic bath and a scented massage every day.
—Hippocrates (c. 460 B.C.–c. 360 B.C.)

The perfume of the beautiful, large ylang ylang flower is so extraordinary that it is known in the Malayan language as the "flower of flowers," which is the literal translation of the flower's name. Generally small, ylang ylang trees are have been known to grow up to one hundred feet in height.

The first oil drawn off in the distillation process is the highest quality and graded "extra," with the trees bearing the smallest flowers producing the subtlest perfume.

Ylang ylang has a balancing effect on blood pressure and distressed breathing patterns. This exotic oil with a heady, sensual fragrance is believed to possess euphoric qualities and is renowned for its restorative powers. Due to its relaxing effect on the nervous system, ylang ylang has been used throughout the centuries as an antidepressant to therapeutically treat stress, frustration, anger, and shock. Its essential oil has been also prescribed for treatment for skin problems, anxiety, depression, and high blood pressure.

This strong floral essential oil can be used in the bath, but use it sparingly due to its heavy scent. Ylang ylang is a perfect compliment to any relaxation ritual, especially on cold or rainy days.

Applications:
❦ *blends well with jasmine, sandalwood, and rose*

Caution: Cananga is an inferior quality passed off as ylang ylang and sold at an inflated price. The oil is often falsified with cocoa butter or coconut oil. To test the oil, place it in the freezer for a short time. If the oil thickens and becomes cloudy, it has been contaminated with additives.

Aromatic Bath

Sweet Ylang Ylang Bath

4 tbsps. sweet almond carrier oil

6 drops ylang ylang essential oil

Run a warm bath. Mix the carrier oil and the essential oil together. Stir well and add to the bath waters just before you enter. Play nature music of the ocean and light a scented candle made with a few drops of ylang ylang essential oil. For a peaceful, midday interlude, blend up a virgin piña colada and take it with you to soak in the fragrant waters.

AROMATIC BATH

This afternoon, treat yourself to an aromatic bath. Since essential oil droplets floating on top of the water may irritate skin and leave red marks, try this simple trick: add seven drops of essential oil to a capful of a mild shampoo and place it under the warm running water just before the tub is full. Also, it is best not to combine more than four essential oils in a tub, keeping the total drops to fewer than twelve for a full bath.

Taking a bath in water that is too hot can be debilitating, so do the old-fashioned water test for babies and use your elbow to test the temperature. To gain the therapeutic benefits of essential oil, soak for a minimum of fifteen minutes. Breathe in deeply and enjoy this application of aromatherapy.

CALMING FACIAL SAUNA

Soak in this exquisite spa treatment once or twice a week. Collect a large ceramic bowl, a luxurious bath towel, and a calming essential oil such as chamomile, which is ideal for both the skin and the mind. To get ready for your spa treatment, boil a pot of water and fill the bowl with it. Let it cool to one hundred degrees Fahrenheit. Add two to three drops of the oil and stir it well with a spoon. Sit in front of your facial sauna and place a towel over your head to create a tent. Close your eyes and lean over the steaming water, but do not get closer than twelve inches. Breathe in deeply through your nose and inhale the vapors for up to five minutes.

SCENTED CANDLES AND INCENSE

The act of lighting a candle deliberately slows the day. The same tranquillity shines true when incense is used for aromatherapy. Gift shops, health, beauty, and grocery stores, as well as street fairs and oriental markets, sell scented candles, incense, burners, and trays to help you experience aromatherapy. Some candles are labeled aromatherapy and deliver the therapeutic benefits of the essential oil, while others use artificial additives to arrive at the named aroma. Do a sniff test to narrow your decision and purchase what your nose likes. I usually buy the smallest candle to make sure the scent, when lit, is what I expected. Also, check to make sure that the wick is made of paper and not lead because the latter is a health hazard.

With incense, experiment with small cones first or buy a single stick. For a safe way to burn incense and allow its aroma to waft through the room, select a metal or ceramic burner with a ventilated lid. Long, thin trays designed of wood or ceramic are a good option for incense sticks or wands. These burners have a pierced opening at the far end to hold the incense at an angle and to capture the falling ash.

Always remember to light a candle or incense stick in a draft-free area away from flammable materials such as curtains, paper, books, magazines, and table linens. Never leave a burning candle or incense wand unsupervised and always blow it out before you nap. Use a candle plate, tray, or holder so as not to mar the surface beneath it or cause a fire. If you trim a candle's wick to ¼ inch before each use, it will last longer and burn evenly.

DIFFUSER

Shop for a diffuser made of metal and glass, ceramic, or terra cotta and discover this easy way to diffuse the essence of ylang ylang into your nap corner. With the simple light of a votive candle, the oil is heated in a small pool of water and released into your room. Watch to make sure the water does not evaporate before the candle burns out.

CERAMIC AMPHORA

This natural, nonaversive diffuser emits a lofty fragrance without using a naked flame or electricity. It is a safe aromatherapy alternative if at the office or children are nearby. Its design is borrowed from ancient Greece and Rome, as an amphora was a two-handled, floor-sized storage jar with an oval body that tapered to a point at the base used for holding wine and oil. Today, these miniature versions of the antique vases appear to be a decorative item to the unknowing eye, yet the ceramic amphora holds a hidden reservoir for release of the calming essence.

REFRESHING CAR FRAGRANCE

For harmony in your car, hang an amphora filled with a brisk essential oil like eucalyptus from the rearview mirror. Another safe way to add aromatherapy is with an auto diffuser. Simply plug the device into the lighter to release the purifying aroma.

SWEET SOUNDS
BY JOHN WILLIAM GODWARD

CHAPTER SEVEN

The Sounds of Sleep

FOUNTAINS, CHIMES, AND MUSIC

We need time to dream, time to remember and time to reach the infinite. Time to be.
—*Gladys Taber (1899–1980)*

Our sense of hearing is almost as strong as our sense of smell. While our memories of olfactory sensations arc important, reminding us of what foods and situations are safe and enjoyable and which are dangerous and poisonous, it is music that calms the spirit and allows balance to return between the mind and body.

The need to have music and peaceful sounds in our lives stems from our earliest days when our mother's heartbeat lulled us. If the percussion of a song is sixty or fewer beats per minute, similar to the sound of a beating heart, its tempo makes for soothing music. All relaxing music has either slow or little percussion. Its tempo of gradual *crescendos* and *decrescendos*, or flowing themes, makes us feel relaxed or even sleepy.

Music with a faster beat, such as rock 'n' roll, marches, anthems, and polkas, makes us feel like dancing or singing instead of napping.

Today, go and discover new music and sleep-inducing sounds to complement your relaxation time.

WATER MUSIC

Gutta cavat lapidem. *(Dripping water hollows out a stone.)*

——Latin saying

The sound of water— gurgling, splashing, rushing, roaring—stirs something primal inside us and comforts us. Inspire calmer moments in your busy days with the promise of a fountain in your nap sanctuary. The deep murmur of a desktop, garden, or patio fountain will play endlessly and instill the body with a sense of peacefulness. To create a focal point in my nap corner, I use fountain adorned with copper that has turned to a verdigris finish. This stunning sculpture actually becomes more beautiful over time when left to the elements. A work of art in itself, the water bell fountain circulates water skyward into a dozen brass cups, the water cascades over the full brims to the small catch pool below, and the bells clink against each other, sending sweet pearls of music into the air.

Explore nurseries, garden shops, import markets, health food shops, and specialty home décor stores to discover the variety of water treasures offered. A fountain pacifies nerves and also humidifies the air at home or at work. Let the water music fill your spirit with a sense of tranquillity and release your mind to roam free from stress and worry.

Tip: *Frequently refill water in fountains to avoid burning out the motor.*

NATURE'S SERENADE

Those who contemplate the beauty of the Earth find reserves
of strength that will endure as long as life lasts.

—*Rachel Louise Carson (1907–1964)*

Music from our feathered friends may be the closest to heavenly song available on this Earth. This summer, create an outside oasis and ensure beautiful natural music with the addition of a birdbath, a birdfeeder, or a wildlife feeder. Nature will gladly sing to us in a melody that is incomparable to any instrument made by our hands.

Lift the mood of an entire afternoon with a birdbath on a balcony or lawn to attract happy singing and splashing or perch a wooden birdhouse in the crook of a tall tree.

Another way to invite nature into your relaxation corner is to add a birdfeeder. Small songbirds will serenade you. If you include a sunflower or thistle feeder, larger beautiful birds will visit your sanctuary.

Consider these suggested types of bird food to attract different types of birds.
black oil sunflower seeds: *goldfinches, nuthatches, and chickadees*
striped sunflower seeds: *blue jays, cardinals, evening grosbeaks, and woodpeckers*
thistle or niger seed: *goldfinches, siskins, and redpolls*
wild bird mix: *chickadees, mockingbirds, titmouses, and other songbirds*
dried or fresh fruit: *American robins and rose-breasted grosbeaks*
Also offer unshelled peanuts to have the bird linger longer at the birdfeeder.

If you live in the country, border a park, or are near a pond, a wildlife feeder will attract swans, geese, and small, friendly, four-legged neighbors. Deer will visit if a salt lick is offered. A clay, ceramic, or wooden toad cottage filled with fresh leaves and grass will invite amphibians into a backyard and create the musical chorus of a pond. As a thank-you for the food and lodging, the frogs will keep pesky insects at bay. Encourage a plethora of beautiful sightings with a hummingbird feeder or a wooden butterfly house. These visits from the wild with their hypnotic songs and incredible colors will surround you in a sense of peace.

ANGELIC SONGS

Happiness lies in the fulfillment of the spirit through the body.
—Cyrol Connolly (1903–1974)

*Recent scientific studies show that the recording of the sound
waves produced by Tibetan bowls replicates the same alpha wave
pattern the brain produces when the body is in a state of relaxation.*

For centuries, bells have been rung regularly in daily lives of people from vastly different cultures. Bells ring for political, spiritual, and religious reasons and as a guiding sound for those on the water, in the fields, or for others looking to the solemn sound for comfort in its repetitive music.

Adopt bells into your nap sanctuary with a modern-day twist on the antique bells from the seaside, hillsides, and fields. Today's Noah or shepherd's bells are rustic bells made of wrought iron and can be sounded with an attached leather strap or a wooden ringer. Available in various sizes, hang several bells from the rafters of a porch or scatter them across a large limb of a grand tree. Signal the start of your nap session *al fresco* and strike each bell. Their music will make the air sing with tranquil tones perfect for reflection.

In my search for the perfect bells, I recently discovered garden bells. This bouquet of brass blossoms makes wonderful music when covered with morning dew or full of raindrops and all it takes to hear their music is a delicate breeze. Place these bells in a flower garden, a potted plant, or in a window box and let their soft sound coax your tired body to take a nap.

Musical wind chimes designed by classically trained musicians will be both an instrument and a piece of art. For years of rich, melodic music, select rustproof aluminum chimes.

Bamboo chimes, with their imported tropical character, can be hung from a patio umbrella or dangled on a shepherd's hook over a flowerbed. Hear their sweet "clink and clank" when swayed by the air current from a ceiling fan or as a breeze drifts across the porch. Surrender to any of these angelic harmonies made by nature—fountains, bells, or chimes—and allow the enchantment of music to fill your afternoon.

INVITE NATURE INDOORS

Silence is the speech of love, the music of the spheres above.
—*Richard Henry Stoddard (1825–1903)*

There is no absolute silence in our world; even earplugs cannot block all sounds. When we close our ears to outside noises, our blood still pulses through our veins, our heart beats constantly, and we hear our breath move in and out. Ancient Greek mathematician, philosopher, and musician Pythagoras believed that the universe is a vast musical instrument and the motion of the planets and the frequencies in life are set to the natural tone of *E*. The purity of these organically occurring vibrations in nature is enchanting, therapeutic, and unconsciously craved by all. While some sounds can stimulate the nervous system in a beneficial way, noise can grate on nerves. Dripping faucets, barking dogs, and screaming car alarms can interfere with getting a sound nap. If you cannot avoid the noise at home or at work, try earplugs or create white noise by running a fan, the air conditioning, or a heater to allow you your well-deserved rest.

Johannes Brahms wrote "Brahms's Lullaby," also known as "Lullaby and Good Night," possibly the most popular sleepy-time song ever composed, yet no one could sleep in the same room with the German composer for he was known for his horrific snoring.

In my search for soothing background sounds, I discovered sound machines. These machines are a wonderful invention and are now finding their way into doctors' offices and work environments to calm anxiety and alleviate stress. With six to twenty nature sound settings, a sound machine can offer restful background options from all over the globe: rolling ocean waves, a bubbling creek, the distant rumble of a waterfall, or the gradual whisper of rain in an approaching thunderstorm—all can soothe the spirit.

HARMONIOUS NOTES

Music makes people kinder, gentler, more staid and reasonable.
—*Martin Luther (1438–1546)*

Venture into a world of new music as you nap, meditate, daydream, or explore your creative spirit. New Age, Celtic, ancient songs, classical, piano solos, jazz, and nature sounds—any selection from this dazzling collection of intriguing music can calm the mind, body, and spirit.

RELEASE IN NEW AGE

Music washes away from the soul the dust of everyday life.
—*Bethold Auerbach (1812–1882)*

New Age music combines influences of Eastern and Western cultures by mixing new and antique instruments. Current-day composers of New Age music can be sampled under such diverse sections as meditation, massage, sacred, sensual, and relaxation.

Research shows that Gregorian chants calm and soothe both the monks chanting as well as those who are listening.

New Age Sounds

A Day without Rain by Enya

Acoustic Planet by Craig Chaquico

Ancient Journey by Cusco

Chant by the Benedictine Monks of Santo Domingo de Silos

Close to Silence by Thomas Otten

Cosmopoly by Andreas Vollenweider

Four Corners by Craig Chaquico

In the Key of Healing by Steven Halpern

Intimacy: Music for Love by Raphael

Mystic Journey by Suzanne Teng

River of Stars by 2002

Seventh Heaven by Govi

The Isle of Dreaming by Kate Price

The Mask and Mirror by Loreena McKennitt

The Reality of a Dreamer by Mythos

Ultimate Massage by Miramar

Vision: The Music of Hildegard von Bingen by Richard Souther

FLOW INTO CELTIC HARMONIES

I first saw a dulcimer played on with sticks knocking the strings, and is very pretty.

—*Samuel Pepys (1633–1703)*

Beginning in the eleventh century, medieval minstrels traveled through southern France writing poems and singing songs of courtly love. This first taste of secular music gave rise to Celtic and other native folk songs throughout Europe. Celtic music is still magical and timeless.

Celtic Harmonies

A Following Wind: Traditional Music from Celtic Shores by Glenn Morgan

Celtic Crossroads: The Uncharted Path by Doug Cameron

Celtic Love Songs by Celtophile

Celtic Moods: Fir na keol by Celtic Collections

Celtic Tides: A Musical Odyssey by Putumayo World Music

Celtic Twilight by various artists

Circle of the Sun by Áine Minague

D is for Dulcimer: Traditional Celtic Music by Glenn Morgan and Jim Wells

Faire Celts: A Woman's Voice by Narada

Southwind: Traditional Celtic Music by Glenn Morgan

Tierra de Nadia by Jose Angel

Traditional Music of Scotland by Celtophile

LISTEN TO ANCIENT VOICES

Let me tell thee, time is a very precious gift of God; so precious that it is only given to us moment by moment.

—*Amelia Barr (1831–1919)*

The civilizations of the ancient Egyptians, the Mayans, the Andeans, the Peruvians, and the Native American Indians all pay tribute to the Earth in their songs.

Ancient Songs

Ancient Egypt by Ali Jihad Racy

Ancient Voices by Anhinga

Apurimac Volume 2: Return to Ancient America by Cusco

Hidden World by Jonn Serrie and Gary Stroutsos

In the Garden of Souls by Vas

Instrumental Dream Volume One by Mehdi

Passion Flute by Stephen DeRuby

Pray by Douglas Spotted Eagle

Sacred Spirit: Chants and Dances of the Native Americans by Sacred Spirit

Shaman by Troika

Spirits of the Canyon by Anhinga

Tao of Healing by Dean Evenson and Li Xiangting

Tribal Meetings, Native American and Andean Flute Music by Anhinga

Under One Sky: Native American Flute and Rhythm by Red Feather Music

Voices by Douglas Spotted Eagle

CLEAR WITH CLASSICAL COMPOSITIONS

Thoughts are energy and you can make your world or break your world by your thinking.

—Susan L. Taylor (b. 1946)

Nadia Boulanger, a French composer and conductor, was considered one of the most influential music teachers of the twentieth century. She guided several generations of American composers.

Classical music, with its deep, sweeping sounds, flowing melodies, and varied chord arrangements, is able to put every human emotion into its notes. Minor notes can sound mysterious. Major keys make us respond with a happy, uplifted feeling. Different meters are used to compose lullabies and waltzes. Woodwind and string instruments, especially, touch our spirits and trigger an emotional response. Symphonies of slow frequencies create an atmosphere of openness and peace that soothes, relaxes, heals, and encourages sleep.

In 1742, Johann Sebastian Bach wrote the Goldberg Variations to relax Count Hermann Karl von Keyserlingk, who was an insomniac.

Researchers at the University of California, Irvine, discovered that listening to classical music before an IQ test can boost scores by as much as nine points and now believe music can help build and strengthen nerve cells in the cerebral cortex.

Classical Sounds

Antonio Vivaldi (1678–1741)—Italian
Johann Sebastian Bach (1685–1750)—Hungarian
Joseph Haydn (1732–1809)—Austrian
Wolfgang Amadeus Mozart (1756–1791)—Austrian
Ludwig Van Beethoven (1770–1827)—German

Franz Schubert (1797–1828)—Austrian

Richard Wagner (1813–1883)—German

Johann Strauss (1825–1899)—Austrian

Igor Stravinksy (1882–1971)—Russian-American

Nadia Boulanger (1887–1979)—French

German composer Clara Weick Schumann, recognized as one of the greatest pianists of all time, had a direct influence on the music of her husband, Robert Schumann, as well as on the compositions of Johannes Brahms.

Exhale with Soft Jazz and Blues

Through music the passions enjoy themselves.

—*Friedrich Nietzsche (1844–1900)*

Every Memorial Day weekend, my husband and I attend a jazz concert that sells out every year at the San Juan Mission in San Juan Capistrano, California, where more than forty musicians gather in the one hundred–year-old courtyard for the twilight event. The evening is always perfect, with superb jazz and blues. Each year I return home with new music to hold me over until the next concert. Why not check the paper and see what local venues are bringing you an opportunity to sample new music?

Soft Jazz

Borrasca by Ottmar Liebert
Chill Factor by Richard Elliot
Dancing Fantasy by Dancing Fantasy
Force Field by 3rd Force
Jazzified by Slim Man
Kind of Blue by Miles Davis
Piece of My Soul by Khani Cole
Paths, Prints by Jan Garbarek
Random Factors by Dino Pacifici
Somethin' 'Bout Love by Brian Culbertson
Journey: The Best of Adiemus by Adiemus

CONNECT TO NATURE

Through woods and mountain passes
the winds, like anthems, roll.
—*Henry Wadsworth Longfellow (1807–1882)*

Nature recordings often combine the sounds of the rainforest, the ocean, or distant wolves with the light notes of a harp, dulcimer, or woodwinds. Many of these tranquil arrangements also have been successfully married to classical symphonies. What a comforting way to enjoy the serenity of nature.

Nature Music

Before the Storm by New Age Music

Duets: Flute / Harp by Compass Productions

Earth Rhythms by various artists

Echoes of Nature: Ocean Waves by Kim Wilson

Loon Song by Nature Quest

Nature's Whispers: Waterfall Suite by Klaus Black and Tini Beier

Ocean Odyssey by Bernie Krause

Sanctuary: Music from a Zen Garden by Riley Lee

Seascapes by Michael Jones

Songs of the Whales: Sounds of Nature by Macheis Wind

Swim with the Dolphins by John St. John

Thunder Magic by Chuck Lange

GIRL READING
BY CHARLES EDWARD PERUGINI

CHAPTER EIGHT

Dedicated to Soothe

ICED AND HOT BEVERAGES

Our sense of taste is a complex and important sensation that allows us to savor foods and beverages and directly affects our moods. Our sense of taste gives life its zest. Enjoy a cool beverage in the warm weather or a soothing cup of hot tea in the crisp weather. The sweetness or tartness will set the tone for a refreshing relaxation.

SOOTHING COLD DRINKS

Any way you whip, blend, or shake up a smoothie of fruit or vegetables, you are drinking to your health. One of my favorite afternoon nap beverages is freshly squeezed orange juice. I purchased an inexpensive electric juicer that can only handle half an orange at a time. The process of juicing itself is therapeutic because you know you are doing something healthy for your body. For a bit of tang, blend a grapefruit or lemon into the fresh mix.

Smoothies are better than soda. Juice drinks and smoothies are good for women on the perpetual go, kids, and moms-to-be. Retire for twenty minutes and sip your vitamins and minerals today. Your body will thank you with better health.

Juice bars have become as ubiquitous as coffee bars and have added frozen drinks to the fast-paced life and menu of Americans. Unlike fast food though, these cold, on-the-run drinks made from fresh or frozen fruit or vegetables are good for you.

Incorporate a frothy frappé into your nap regime. Go sweet with a frozen blend of mango, pineapple, and kiwi or venture to the other side of the farm and whip up a drink made from veggies.

A light snack, a meal, or a decedent dessert, these iced treats can be made with a host of mixers. Soy, rice, almond milk, yogurt, ice cream, sherbet, gelato, juice, milk, or even just water and ice can be used as a base. The only rule is that you must drink it fresh. In other words, taste it immediately to thoroughly enjoy its flavor and intended consistency.

Add a fancy straw, a decorative stirrer, or a tiny paper Japanese umbrella and spice up your prenap drink.

Garnishes for Fruity Drinks	Garnishes for Veggie-Based Beverages
whipped cream	jalapenos
chocolate shavings	Worchester sauce
nutmeg	cucumber slices
cinnamon stick	asparagus spear
lemon twist	black or green olives
berries	celery seeds
papaya spear	lime wedge
frozen juice ice cubes	carrot stick
frozen ice cubes with fruit	cocktail onions
tiny marshmallows	Tabasco sauce

HOLIDAY AND SEASONAL DRINKS

For a new spin on potential beverages for your nap, consider drinks traditionally whipped up around the holidays or when the seasons change, such as spicy cider, hot cocoa in hazelnut, white chocolate or mint flavors, eggnog, cranberry, or spiced orange glögg.

Scandinavian Spiced Orange Glögg

4 cups white grape juice

2 cups orange juice

¼ cup brown sugar

1 tsp cardamom

⅛ tsp ginger

Combine the orange juice and the spices in a nonaluminum pot. Slowly heat to a boil, stirring occasionally. Add the grape juice, stir, and serve while warm.

Drink from the Fountain of Youth

A life without water would be very short indeed. We cannot survive without the drink of life, so be sure to include pure, fresh water as part of your napping regimen. Jazz those water afternoons up a bit and try sparkling or noncarbonated mineral water. Make your own soda—pour your favorite juice and top it off with a little sparkling water to make a not-too-sweet beverage or look for the Italian and Canadian imported sodas. Pour a highball glass of soda or club water and garnish it with a citrus twist, slice, or wedge. Keep a carafe of water beside you while you relax. Throughout the day, be sure to drink the recommended eight glasses of water.

HOT BEVERAGES TO SIP

Better to be deprived of food for three days than of tea for one.

—*ancient Chinese saying*

Tea transcends time and culture. Chinese Emperor Shen Nung always boiled his water before drinking it because he had observed that those who did had better health. As the legend claims, sometime in 2737 B.C., his servants made a fire from the branches of a nearby tree and as the water began to boil, some of the topmost leaves fell into the water. Intrigued by the aroma, the emperor sipped the steaming liquid, declared it wonderful, and called his new beverage the "Divine Healer." According to the Chinese, this was the discovery of tea.

The Japanese tea ceremony is called cha-no-yu, *or "hot water for tea."*
The rules of the tea ceremony, written hundreds of years ago, prescribe the act in extreme detail: the room, tea, utensils, decorations, and all movements. Guests kneel on tatami *mats, receive the tea bowl, sip the delicate liquor reflectively with the host, and discover the four principles of the ceremony: harmony, respect, purity, and tranquillity.*

In 1614, tea first arrived in France. It was considered a drug and was therefore only sold in pharmacies. The custom of taking milk with tea began in London around 1630. Prior to that time, Europeans tried tea with other additives including saffron, salt, ginger, and nutmeg. The English liked their tea with either oysters or clams. The Germans poured beer into it. The Irish mixed in whiskey and for the Italians and Spaniards, onions and garlic were regular additives. The Russians splashed champagne into their tea. In the United States, New Yorkers preferred a dollop of ice cream in their tea and the true Bostonians added rose leaves. Serve and drink your tea any way you like it. As you can see, there is truly no right or wrong manner.

Tea Tip: Rose petals floated on top of brewed tea offer a light and spicy-sweet taste, but only use the most fragrant blooms and pinch off all of the white heels of the petals to eliminate any bitterness.

THE AMERICAN CONTRIBUTION

Lemon verbena, a most flavorful lemon herb, is a great garnish for tea—iced or served hot. Lemon balm and lemon geranium are also known to calm the spirit.

America has made two big contributions to tea-drinking history: iced tea and the tea bag. Iced tea was introduced at the Louisiana Purchase Exposition in 1904, when exhibitor Richard Blechynden, an Englishman and tea dealer, wanted to introduce black tea from India. Out of sheer desperation in the record-breaking heat of St. Louis that summer, Blechynden poured his tea over ice and served the cool, copper-colored liquid in tall glasses. Today in the United States, more than 80 percent of those who drink tea prefer it over ice.

The same year, the tea bag was introduced. New York tea merchant Thomas Sullivan, in a savvy marketing ploy, sent customers samples of tea in little silk pouches. To his surprise, orders for the convenient tea bags poured in when people discovered how simple it was to make tea in this new way.

Tea Tip: Place a clove in the center of a lemon pinwheel slice and float it on top of afternoon tea for additional aroma and flavor.

This universal drink, called by many similar words—tea, *tee*, *te*, *thé*, *cha*, and *chai*—is more than an enjoyable beverage. All teas are reported to be high in vitamin C and can aid in digestion. Tea can also contain vitamins B_1, B_2, K, and P. When this fascinating plant's leaves are brewed and sipped, many claim it aids in the restoration of balance and tranquillity. Served without milk, sugar, or honey, tea has no calories or fat content and contains hidden extra nutritional benefits such as manganese, potassium, niacin, and folic acid. In fact, a cup of black tea has fifty-eight milligrams of potassium.

Recently, researchers at the University of Purdue concluded that a compound in green tea inhibits the growth of cancer cells.

Recent studies have shown that drinking green tea may even protect against heart disease, improve immunity, inhibit cancerous cell growth, and prevent tooth decay due to its bacteria-destroying properties. The only downside to sipping tea is that green tea has approximately thirty-five milligrams of caffeine, oolong has fifty, and black tea has about one hundred and ten milligrams (a cup of coffee averages one hundred and seventy-five milligrams). Only herbal infusions and the new red teas allow those with sensitivity to caffeine to enjoy a cup without any stimulating side effects.

Tea Tip: *Select a teapot made from glass, ceramic, or stainless steel. Never use aluminum or iron. The same advice applies to the kettle used to boil the water.*

Your teatime ritual can be as simple as dipping a tea bag into a mug or as elaborate as a Victorian tea. Accoutrements such as hand-decorated sugars, little filigree sugar tongs, scones, lemon curd, Devonshire cream, imported tea leaves presented in beautiful, soldered tin boxes, and a sterling silver ball to dip into an antique teapot are arcane niceties of traditional tea etiquette. If you opt to go the mug-and-tea-bag route, take the extra five minutes to boil the water on the stove-top rather than using the quick fix in the microwave. Ritual is what your soul needs to experience, not fast-food tea. While you wait for the pot of tea to boil, turn off the phone and do something completely and only for you. Page through an art book, write in your journal, read a book of poetry, meditate, or stretch a bit and try a new yoga position. Smile because you know this moment is just for you.

Tea Tip: The quality of your water will determine the quality of your tea. Since many locales have tasteable sulfur, minerals, or chlorine in their water, use filtered or bottled water for your tea water.

BREWING OPINIONS

The word "teaspoon" originated in its use for measuring the amount of tea leaves to go into the pot.

Some tea traditionalists say that before you start, bag the bag, along with those tea balls. Loose tea is messy, hence the saying, "the agony of the leaves," but connoisseurs proclaim that the authentic, heavenly flavor released as the leaves swirl deliriously and unrestrained in boiling water is the only true way to find such divinity on Earth.

The reason that these tea aficionados abhor the tea bag is because the quality of tea generally used in tea bags is not very high. However, in recent years, several of the major tea companies have vastly improved the reputation of the tea bag, packaging such flavors as Earl Grey, Darjeeling, and English Breakfast in convenient bags. So, I say tea bags can be embraced as an ideal way to sample new teas without shame. Once you have found a tea you really savor, you might want to buy a small quantity in bulk and experiment with the loose leaves.

Tea Tip: After time and use, an unglazed teapot will absorb the flavors of the tea. Use one pot for one type of tea: red, herbal, oolong, green, and black, or purchase a teapot with a glazed interior to prevent the absorption.

According to the British, "One heaping teaspoon of tea leaves for each cup—and one more for the pot." My experience has shown that the extra teaspoon for the pot can make the tea taste bitter and feel heavy in the mouth. Experiment with what works best for your taste buds. You may find that "less is more."

Tea Tip: Some tea connoisseurs claim that milk clouds the flavor of tea and recommend not to add any. You be the judge.

HANDLE WITH CARE

Tea Tip: Japanese grocery stores have the most interesting teapots and cups at the best prices. Take a detour on the way home to search for these authentic oriental treasures.

Tea is fragile and should be kept in a dark, cool place, but not the refrigerator or freezer. Black tea without flowers or fragrances can keep up to one year. Scented teas will last about three to five months. Store in an airtight, waterproof, and opaque container such as ceramic containers, mason jars with clamp lids, or high-quality tins for protection against tea's mortal enemies: dampness, heat, and light.

Tea Tip: Instead of sweetening tea with refined white sugar, try honey, raw sugar, brown sugar, maple syrup, or even molasses.

Tips for the Perfect Cup

- First, swish hot water inside the teapot or set it on a sunny spot on the windowsill. Once the pot is warm to the touch, discard the water.
- Use one teaspoon of tea per one six-ounce serving of water.

- If you have selected a tea with herbs and flowers, gently crush the leaves and petals into the pot to release the flavorful oils.
- Pour freshly boiled water over the tea leaves and cover them. This will saturate the tea to extract its flavors. According to the type of tea you are making, brew for three to five minutes.
- If you can smell your tea while steeping it, you are losing your medicine. Cover the pot with a tea towel, including the spout. If you are using a mug, cover the top with a saucer.

Tea Tip: Steeping tea too long may produce a bitter taste.

If Using a Tea Bag

- Follow the same instructions as you would if making tea from leaves. Warm the pot or the mug and use freshly boiled water. Infuse the bag for three to five minutes, depending on the type of tea you are brewing.
- Remove the bag with a spoon and allow only the excess tea to drip back into the cup. Do not squeeze or wring the bag into the cup because it will only deposit a bitter residue. Never use a tea bag twice. Tea made from a secondhand tea bag will taste stale and lifeless.

Tea Tip: Use a wooden box, gold wire, or woven wicker basket or a wooden or silver tray to hold everything for teatime: tea boxes and tins, your favorite cup or mug, cinnamon and honey sticks, tea ball, strainer, and tea books.

ON BECOMING A TEA CONNOISSEUR

All told, there are more than three thousand varieties of tea and, just like wines, they take their names from the districts where they are grown. About 70 percent of the tea that Americans drink each year comes from India, Indonesia, Sri Lanka (Ceylon), Kenya, Malawi, and Tanzania. Tea plants flourish where it is warm, in tropical or subtropical climates. Where there is a great deal of rainfall and at altitudes between three thousand and seven thousand feet, the finest teas are produced.

Tea tasting is an art. The masters are able to identify between fifteen hundred and sixteen hundred different types of teas and can tell where the leaf was grown, its variety, the season when the leaves were picked, and the drying process. Teas are categorized according to when they are harvested: First Flush (April–May), In Between (May–June), Second Flush (June–August), and Autumn (November–December).

Begin your tea adventure by sampling a new herbal infusion and then try a red tea, a green, and an oolong. If you are caffeine-sensitive, only drink black tea upon awakening or in place of coffee. Once you have tasted enough varieties to have a preference for one or another, you will be on your way to becoming a true tea expert.

*The English, adamant about their tea, never use soap when cleaning the pot;
they simply rinse and set it to dry so as to preserve the flavoring.*

HERBAL INFUSIONS

Wonderfully aromatic, these light and refreshing beverages—herbal teas, tisanes, or infusions, as they are called—can be enjoyed before a nap because they contain no caffeine. Such concoctions are made with stems, roots, tree barks, grasses, leaves, berries, seeds, and fruits of various plants, as well as with zesty citrus peels, and can be laced with sweet and spicy accents of flowers. Add an orange twist to a tall glass of herbal iced tea or top off a steaming cup of tea with a sprinkle of cinnamon.

Hibiscus Rose Hips

Hibiscus rose hip tea is delightful in the winter as a "warmer-upper" or in the summertime when it is sipped as an iced drink. Add a little honey and a squeeze of lemon, orange, or lime to this rich, burgundy tea.

Ginseng Tea

The Chinese character for the ginseng leaf, *sou*, represents the ancient symbol for immortality. Although it is caffeine free, drinking this infusion is believed to spark a renewal of energy.

Tea Tip: Herbal teas are generally light in color, so brewing them longer will not make them darker.

Egyptian Chamomile

This tisane of only the flowers of this calmative herb produces a healthy body with a fresh scent reminiscent of green apples.

Lemon

This delightful infusion's predominant aroma is derived from lemon grass.

Verveine Odorante (Lemon Verbena)

Imported from France, these big, green leaves produce a full-bodied brew with a calming influence.

Peppermint

This is a peppy tea without caffeine that can naturally soothe the stomach.

Fruit Teas

A delicate mixture of fruit and leaves, herbal fruit offers a variety of flavors: apricot, raspberry, peach, spiced plum, cinnamon apple, mango, black currant, passionfruit, cranberry, or citrus blends.

Tilleul de Carpentras (Linden Tree Tea)

Grown in the picturesque French village province of Carptentras, a cup of Tilleul de Carpentras is exquisite, with a light, woodsy, and subtle flavor. I special-ordered this tea and found it worth the wait.

Rooibos

A red, herbal tea fairly new to reach the United States, this mahogany-colored beverage contains no caffeine, is low in tannins, and rich in essential minerals. Note: rooibos is a very rich tea and only one tea bag is needed for two or three cups.

GREEN TEA

Revered for its health benefits, green tea has been a mainstay in China and Japan for thousands of years. Green tea has a lighter taste and less caffeine than black tea.

Green tea contains the antioxidant ECGE, a compound twenty times more effective than vitamin E, two hundred times as powerful as vitamin C, and believed to reduce the risk of cancer.

Sencha

Sencha is the popular green tea that the Japanese drink every day. A very delicate brew and golden in color, sencha tea has a sweet aroma and an excellent flavor. Try Chinese sencha and organic sencha to compare the differences.

Gyokuro

Gyokuro is Japan's finest green tea that pours out in a bright green color and delivers an intense flavor.

Genmaicha

During the drying process of genmaicha, rice kernels are added. The finished result is a liquor of amber with floating rice and an intriguing roasted flavor.

Lung Ching

Highly esteemed by the Chinese, this tea has a delicate vegetative flavor, which is also slightly sweet. Also called Dragon Well or Ling Ching, it pours out to a pale emerald green in color, delivering a fragrant aroma and a sweet taste.

Gunpowder Green

The large, grayish-green leaves of this green tea are rolled into pellets. Delivered in what resembles lead shot, it is often infused with fresh mint or lemon leaves. Its thin, pale, slightly bitter liquor contradicts its belligerent name. The Chinese also call it Pearl Tea, due to its wondrous and smooth taste. Be brave and try Gunpowder. Note: you will need less tea than normal to make a pot.

Jasmine Blossom Green Tea

This large-leafed, semifermented tea has been a favorite of the Chinese since the Sung Dynasty, which ruled more than eight hundred years ago. Flavored with jasmine blossoms that expand beautifully in the teapot, its aroma is heavenly.

China White Tea

A rare tea produced only in China, this infusion of the silver-dotted, needle-like white leaves pours out in a pale yellow brew with a mellow, sweet taste. White teas are ideal iced during summertime for they are known to reduce the body's temperature. China White Tea, considered a type of a green tea, is often sold as Yin Zhen, Silvery Tip Pekoe, China White, or Fujian White.

Tea Tip: When preparing water for tea, remove it from the heat as soon as it boils. If left to continue boiling, the water will lose oxygen and the tea will taste flat.

OOLONG TEA

The literal translation of *oolong* is "black dragon," referring to its dark, twisted tea leaves. Known for its rich flavor, bright color, and orchid-like fragrance, oolong tea is popular in many Chinese restaurants in the United States and south China.

Oolong has a lower amount of caffeine than black teas.

Formosa Oolong

This Chinese tea possesses the exquisite flavors of ripe peaches. Grown on the island of Formosa, now called Taiwan, it is the most expensive tea from this area. Also try Oolong Imperial (considered the best of the Formosa oolong teas), Tung Ting (another favorite that offers a mild taste), or Ti Kuan (amber in color, with a delicate, flowery taste).

Fenghuang Shuixian

This exceptional tea is picked from a plant that has been allowed to grow into a tree. These very large leaves surprisingly still permit a full, yet gentle flavor. The pale green tea can be infused several times with each cup providing a finely different tasting experience.

Ti Quan Yin

One of China's most famous teas, this oolong delivers a full aroma with a medium body. Ti Quan Yin is commonly made by the *gongfu* method, which uses tiny pots and requires several infusions.

In 1998, a Harvard University study found that drinking one cup of black tea a day lowered the risk of heart attack by as much as 44 percent.

BLACK TEA

Black tea leaves, when brewed, give a deep, amber liquid with a malt flavor. India produces black teas noted for their delicate bouquet and rich, full-bodied flavor. The best-known gardens are those in the Darjeeling and Assam areas. The list below will help you appreciate the flavor, fragrance, and color of several black teas worth your time tasting.

Darjeeling Tea

The "champagne of teas," Darjeeling offers a delicate, wine-like muscatel flavor with a distinct aroma of black currants. Also described as flowery, this tea is grown on the slopes of the Himalayas and possesses a velvety smooth flavor, beautiful amber color, and exquisite taste.

Tea Tip: According to a recent report in Runners World, *drinking brewed tea, not canned or instant, prevents skin cancer.*

Assam

Assam tea produced in northern India is a superb hot beverage for foul weather and wintry days. It is dark in color, delivers a piquant taste, and is best served with milk.

Ceylon

Grown at high altitudes, this tea is labeled Ceylon even though the area in which it is now cultivated is called Sri Lanka. The most respected Ceylon teas are Eliya, High Forest, Nuwara, Saint James, and Uva Highlands. All variations offer a fine, refreshing flavor with a bright and steady liquid that turns an attractive golden color when milk is added.

CLASSIC BLACK TEA BLENDS

The following black teas are blends created by combining the best leaves for a desired balance of flavor.

English Breakfast

A frequently requested tea, English Breakfast can be a blend of good quality Ceylon and Indian leaves or 100 percent Keemun. While its name may suggest only sipping it at breakfast, be assured that this tea is ideal for any time of the day. Add a touch of milk to this full-bodied and stimulating old-time favorite.

Irish Breakfast

A cup of Irish Breakfast tea offers a rich, rousing cup more so than the English Breakfast tea because of its high proportion of Assam. It is most delicious when served with milk.

Tea Tip: Add a teaspoon of maple syrup to your cup of English or Irish Breakfast tea to make a special autumn treat.

Earl Grey

Wildly popular, Earl Grey is a combination of oriental black teas delicately scented with bergamot essential oil. The essence is expressed from the rind of an unusual, pear-shaped, Mediterranean citrus fruit to give this tea its smooth and aromatic taste.

Chai Spice

In India, chai is a traditional black tea blended with exotic spices, boiled milk, and water to create an invigorating beverage. Its fragrant and spicy aroma of ginger, cinnamon, allspice, nutmeg, clove, and cardamom lingers from sip to sip.

Chinese Black Teas

Black teas from China tend to be lighter and contain less tannin than Indian teas. These black teas have histories that go back hundreds of years. Sample any Chinese black teas from Anhui, Fujian, or Yunnan provinces.

Keemun

Keemun black teas, light and slightly perfumed, from the Anhui province, are first class. Called the "Imperial Tea of China," this tea delivers a clean, delicate taste with a fruity sweetness.

Lapsang Souchoung

This is one of my favorites, a bracing tea that tastes of wood smoke with a lingering pungency. This vigorous, open-aired tea has a bright color like whiskey and, like whiskey, has been known to make its imbiber very cheerful. One word of caution: never add milk to Lapsang Souchoung.

Noon-Day Rest
By John William Godward

CHAPTER NINE

Truly Lavish Essentials

TACTILE COMFORTS FOR INDULGING

Touch is as essential as sunlight.
—*from* A Natural History of the Senses *by Diane Ackerman (b. 1948)*

Touch is as essential to us as our breath. Experts claim that our sense of touch is ten times stronger than verbal contact. Our entire body registers the sense. Our skin is an amazing organ with unique abilities to breathe, resist water, automatically regulate its temperature, and constantly renew every fifteen to thirty days.

Pleasure materials such as silk, cashmere, mohair, and velvet are what our tactile sensation craves. Worry beads, worry dolls, polished stones and pebbles, stress balls, and other palm-sized objects can be used to calm anxieties. This repeated stimulation of touching or rubbing causes our brain waves to slow, lowers our blood pressure, and makes us feel better.

The expression, "His heart touched mine," now has new meaning. William Collinge, M.D.H., Ph.D., in his book Subtle Energy, *writes, "When two subjects held hands, their heartbeats were detectable on each other's skin and in their brain waves. When seated three feet apart and not touching, the electrocardiogram still measured the heart energy waves on both body surfaces.*

Color Matters

*Up the canyon rose far hills and peaks, the big foothills, pine covered and remote.
And far beyond, like clouds upon the border of the sky, towered minarets of white,
where the Sierra's eternal snows flashed austerely the blazes of the sun…
the drifting sound and drifting color seemed to weave together in the making
of a delicate and intangible fabric, which was the spirit of the place.*
—*from "All Gold Canyon" by Jack London (1876–1916)*

The human eye can see approximately seven million different variations of colors.

About 80 percent of the information we assimilate through our senses is with our eyes. Color gives us objective information about our world every day, but it also influences how we feel. Studies in color theory have shown that soft shades of blue and green appease the nervous central system, while bright hues, especially from the red spectrum, can actually accelerate it. Color is important and even though the eyes are shut when napping, sometimes it is getting to that point that is the most difficult. Consider the colors of your linens and sleeping clothing carefully.

Pink, a tranquilizing color, zaps energy. Evidence shows that pink walls will calm violent prisoners, but only for the short term. In 1991, the University of Hawaii's football team noticed that the visiting locker rooms at both Iowa and Colorado State were painted pink. The Western Athletic Conference has now ruled that the visiting team locker room must be painted the same color as the home team's. In the world of napping, however, the color pink is still a perfect choice to encourage a short siesta.

Blue, labeled the universal color for relaxation, is a very good choice for a new set of pajamas. Nearly all cultures describe shades of blue as cooling, calming, and soothing. Surround your-self in blue, the true colors of our sky and oceans. Cover your bed, chair, or nap room in the calming colors of azure, cerulean, indigo, cobalt, rain, corn blue, royal blue, navy, denim, or chambray blue.

The color purple—lavender and violet—a distant cousin of blue, is considered a sign of flamboyance in some cultures, yet possesses religious and magical connotations in others.

Green, another predominant color of the earth, is believed by many to encourage growth and spark new beginnings. Pale green is often perceived as a sign of renewal, as such are the first sprouts of spring. The Egyptians equated green with hope.

The color green is said to be the most restful color for the human eye, possesses healing power, and can soothe pain. People work more effectively when they can see houseplants and patients recovered from surgery faster and with fewer drugs when in a room with a green view.

In London, when the Blackbriar's Bridge was painted green, suicides dropped 34 percent.

Paint your nap room in soothing colors of celery or cucumber. Cool a sunny room with the deep shade of emerald. Jade is considered to represent wisdom and might be a good accent color to bring into a hobby room where the growth of a creative endeavor can be encouraged.

White, symbolic of simplicity and cleanliness, is reserved for spiritual authority in many cultures. In India, if a married woman wears white without a touch of another color, she is believed to be inviting widowhood and unhappiness. A white frost sends us marching for the warmest blanket and slippers in the house.

Most so-called whites are very light grays, but the good news is that the color gray actually calms as well. Even freshly fallen snow, which appears to be purely white, only reflects about 80 percent of the incident light. (To be considered completely white, it would have to reflect 100 percent.) An all-white sanctuary may look elegant, but due to its reflective quality, too much white can overwhelm the eyes and the emotions. Look for soothing shades of whites and select a lightweight blanket woven in almond, ivory, cream, parchment, taupe, or sand. Any linen colored in sophisticated grays is also a safe bet.

At naptime, nothing will feel better than a pair of warm white socks right out of the dryer.

The opposite of white, black, which lacks hues and brightness and absorbs all light without reflecting it, is present in all colors. Black has a grounding effect. Use the color black sparingly in your nap corner. As with white, it has a tendency to overpower the emotions and cause a melancholy response.

"Historically, red is the most energizing color because it's perceived to be a vibrant, hot color," says Leatrice Eiseman, author of Colors for Your Every Mood.

Red, associated with fire and warmth, is the action color of leadership. Since both red and orange have a tendency to make the heart race and excite the nervous system, hues from this side of the color wheel are not recommended in a nap sanctuary, as a primary shade in linens, or on sleep apparel.

Yellow, the color of a bright lemon, is the most fatiguing because it results in excessive stimulation of the eyes. It is the first color the eye is attracted to and is the reason cautionary road signs and some fire engines are painted in yellow. Babies cry more frequently in a room painted yellow, more fights happen in kitchens of this bright hue, and using yellow legal pads might give you an initial jolt, but can become an eye irritant after a while. Use yellow sparingly in your nap area, linens, and apparel, or use softer hints of this sun-color to paint an art studio or bathroom.

Color therapy, the art of applying colors in your life, can make you feel good. For a tranquil nap environment, select solid neutral earth colors, jewel tones, off-whites, blues and greens, or softly patterned designs, so as not to revive up your system. Robes and pajamas in pale pinks and light shades of purple will also complement this peaceful time. Aesthetic is an important factor when purchasing new linens and nap apparel, but still choose by touch. Our sense of touch rarely makes a mistake.

SLEEPWEAR

Semper gestare subcula. *(Always wear underwear.)*
—Latin saying

Today, we have a plethora of napping apparel options. Our "loungewear," a cross between nightwear and sportswear, is appropriate attire for a lazy Saturday afternoon or a trip to the corner store.

According to apparel publications, pajamas have evolved into what the industry has coined "lifestyle dressing." From the basic sweats once issued to members by athletic clubs to collared and button-down tailored pajama sets, anything now works for a nap.

If you decide to nap au natural, *the Better Sleep Council advises that you keep your nap room between the ideal sleeping temperatures of sixty and sixty-five degrees Fahrenheit. A hot room or too many blankets can upset sleep and even cause nightmares.*

Spring and Summertime Textures

Reach for your favorite robe and you will get the huge hug you deserve every time it is tied around your waist. Just like those who choose to lounge around the Mediterranean on holiday, you too might decide that a weighty and absorbent spa robe made from thick-combed Aegean cotton is what your naptime needs. Check the labels to see if the robe you are considering is from Denizli, Turkey—the same place where the world's finest towels are made. These robes, hailed as the crown jewel for pampering, are also incomparable.

Most robes are woven with fourteen ounces of cotton, but your skin will want the incredibly luxurious ones created with twenty-two ounces. The way to tell the difference is to feel the robe for a likeness of an extra thick, king-sized bath towel. These easy-care robes become softer as the cotton fibers bloom with each washing.

SILKY SECRETS

Silk has been woven in China since 1,000 B.C.

For more than three thousand years in China, the cultivation and fabric manufacturing of silk was a guarded secret. Legend claims that two monks smuggled seeds of the mulberry tree and silkworm eggs out of China by hiding them in their walking sticks. India only learned of the secrets of silk when an Indian prince married a Chinese princess.

Any pajama set or robe made of silk is a wonderful nap choice. For ease of care, buy washable silk.

Tip: Silk pillowcases will prevent bed wrinkles on your face and will not muss your hair style.

Silk Kimonos

A featherweight, Japanese kimono-style robe is a regal coat. Try it on with a pair of wooden clogs with a thong that passes between the big toe and the second toe—called *geta*. You might want a pair of *tabi*, the split-toed socks which are worn with this traditional Japanese footwear. Walking in your new shoes will slow your stride and allow stress to race on ahead.

Silky Sheets

In 1572, while still in her teens, Margaret of Valois, the daughter of the strong-willed Queen Catherine de Médicis and King Henry II of France, married the Protestant Henry de Bourbon King of Navarre. To show off her creamy, white skin to its greatest advantage, she apparently demanded and slept on the world's first black satin sheet.

The thread count of sheets, ranging from one hundred and eighty to five hundred plus, determines the fabric's quality and softness. As a general rule of thumb, the higher the count, the better the linens, however, the price of these wonderful sheets goes up with the count. Linen bedding, a bit more expensive, is also a good decision because it lasts a lifetime. It does not retain moisture the way cotton does and will keep you cool in the summer. Silk bedding makes for wonderful year-round sound sleep, cool in the summer and warm in the winter. You may never sleep on anything else again.

COTTON OPTIONS

One of the pleasures of 100 percent cotton sheets is how the fabric gets softer and softer with regular use and washing. Combed cotton knit sheets, called T-shirt or jersey sheets, are softer than percale, cooler than flannel, and do not need ironing. Its stretchy, "give and take" makes it an ideal choice to wrap around you because it fits more snugly than any other woven sheet. Look for the fine-gauge jersey comprised of five ounces of cotton per square yard to deliver a more substantial weight and durability.

To keep your bedding smelling sweet, especially in the summer, scent your sheets and pillowcases by adding lavender or rosemary laundry rinse water to the wash.

Since it is natural to perspire in your sleep, the more natural the bed linen is, the better it is for your health. Avoid synthetics, especially for use on the bed, because these fabrics do not breathe. Finer grades of cotton, woven in a thread count of two hundred and fifty or higher, can add extra fluff to your sanctuary. Now each nap, spent under an umbrella of comforting cotton, will grant your spirit immediate solace.

For those with sensitive skin, sheets, pajamas, and a robe made from organic cotton or hemp are a good idea. This "green" breathable natural fabric is carefully handled without bleach or chemical treatments and is friendly to your skin and the environment.

SCRAPBOOKS OF FABRIC

Even though the art of making quilts began in Europe, it truly flourished in the New World after 1760. Quilts have been as American as apple pie, baseball, the cowboy, and jazz and have experienced a great revival. Many claim that the quintessential American quilt is the repeating block format called the "log cabin." Others favor design themes inspired by nature, such as the flying geese quilt, a triangular-pieced design, which dates back to the early 1800s. The wedding ring quilt is still given to newlyweds and handmade heirlooms are also presented as baby or christening gifts.

The German immigrants who populated southeastern Pennsylvania quilted in mystical hex symbols to protect them in their new homeland and also incorporated nonrepeating symbols such as a red heart for love, tulips for charity, faith, and hope, and green accents to ensure happiness and luck.

Ask about the designs when considering the purchase of a new or antique gem. The stories behind the handiwork are worth the price for the piece of history that you take home. Good to use as picnic blanket and for a siesta afterwards, a quilt will bring comfort, warmth, and a sense of safety to any nap nook.

Wonderful Wool

Wool, one of the cleverest fabrics and most popular fabric for blankets, is cool in summer and warm in winter. There are approximately two hundred different types of varying grades of wool produced by forty different breeds of sheep.

Cashmere goats, raised in central Asia, north India, and Iran, are valued for the wool of their downy undercoat, which makes a spectacular pair of pajamas, a luxurious robe, or a shawl that can be also easily used as a blanket. The extra-fine wool of merino sheep is also known for its softness and durability. Lamb's wool blankets were once primarily created at small mills for generations. Angora goats, native to Asia Minor, are one of the most numerous breeds in the southwest United States and Texas. Silky and feather-light to the fingertips, mohair blankets, made entirely of wool or combined with silk or cotton, are artfully created on a shuttle loom. One touch of any of these woven treasures and you will know that you have made a wise investment. Enjoy, and expect these cherished wraps to last a long time.

Mohair velvet, once used on the chairs in first-class carriages of early trains, is still a beautiful, practical, and durable fabric. Consider reupholstering an old overstuffed chair and matching ottoman in this sumptuous fabric or pick up a few decadent pillows in mohair velvet.

Plaids

In Gaelic, the word "plaid" means "blanket" and describes the shawl worn by the working class and the poor. The wealthy would only wear them for farming and hunting. Fashion experts credit Queen Boadicea of Iceni with donning the first plaid attire. In the first few years of the new millennia B.C., the Egyptians wore sheaths and *schentis* with plaid designs. Scottish clans claim to trace plaids as far back as the sixth century A.D.

Woolen textiles from the early Bronze Age have been found in Scandinavia and Switzerland.

Strictly Cashmere

Elegant napwear is available at a price. Cashmere, no longer reserved just for sweaters, has arrived in pajamas with matching robes. This yarn from Kashmir goats of distant India is spun into the finest down, so the pants fit loosely and a sleeveless chemise will caress your body. Now, imagine slipping into the sensual coziness of a knitted pajama set created from this decadent wool. Feel the additional luxury of a complementary, calf-length robe.

MODERN FABRICS

Blankets and robes made from a new techno-fabric called fleece are also worth trying. Made of easy-to-care-for polyester, its double-sided velour finish will wick away moisture and dry quickly.

In 1953, the first commercial production of the polyester fiber was by the E.I. du Pont de Nemours & Company, Incorporated of the United States. Today, polyester is the most-used synthetic fiber in the United States.

FLANNELS

Another way to add instant warmth to a chilly afternoon is to pull out a pair of flannel pajamas. A tailored shirt and pant set, boxers, a roomy nightgown, or a plaid robe will bring up your core temperature in no time. Should the arctic winds begin to blow where you live, test out the idea of a hooded flannel sleeper. Scientific studies show that body heat escapes through the head, so as a good preventive measure, select a robe or pajamas with a hood.

Most stores carry flannel bed sets made with four ounces of cotton per square yard; however, what you really want to find are the sheets made with five ounces or more. These linens will be warmer and even more comforting than the lighter versions. Choose flannel sheets brushed on both sides and be content in unmatched warmth.

IMPORTED COMFORT

Another warm afternoon nap option is to wrap in the familiarity of chenille. This retro fabric is making a comeback in blankets, bathrobes, and slippers. The French word *chenille* means caterpillar and when the fabric first emerged, it was most commonly used as a bedspread. Today's chenille blankets come in a beautifully textured honeycomb weave.

LONG JOHNS

Grandma used to call them "thermals," Grandpa called them his "union suit," and some areas of the country call long underwear "longies." Today's market offers long johns in an excellent high-tech fabric meant for wicking moisture away from the skin during winter activities, but these long-sleeve tops with matching bottoms are another ideal way to stay warm under the covers at naptime, too. If you're feeling nostalgic, order a red union suit of 100 percent rib-knit cotton with a nine-button placket front and the infamous one-button "drop seat." To eliminate the chance of any backdoor drafts, order the modernized, two-piece set instead.

REGAL NAPPING

Another intriguing idea to replace the standard robe is what men sported to entertain company at home. During the roaring twenties, smoking jackets became the rage. Bring back a stylish piece of the past and enjoy a piece of solitude in your new smoking jacket, or bed jacket, which is shortened at the waist to flatter a woman's body. Dressed quite regally from your overstuffed chair and ottoman, light several candles instead of a cigarette and take a mental vacation to Central Park and Rockefeller Center.

EXTRA FLUFF

Pillows have been with us since the time of the Crusaders, who used these indispensable items for comfort.

Today, we have a tendency to treat pillows as a nice sofa decoration rather than a source of comfort, yet the secret to a truly good nap could be in your pillow. You may never see what is inside a pillow, but you sure can feel the difference that the fill makes with every siesta. Those naturally filled with down or goose feathers will offer the most comfort and long-term performance and will squish to your unique contour and sleeping posture. If you are allergic, consider a hypoallergenic pillow instead of naturally filled ones.

To test a down or feather pillow, fold it in half on a hard, flat surface. (Fold a king-sized pillow into thirds.) Press the air out of it and release. If the pillow does not return to its original shape, it is time to get a new one. To test a polyester pillow, put a hardcover book (about ten ounces) on the folded pillow and let go. It should throw the book and return to its original shape. If not, go out and treat yourself.

Do a visual test to check if the stuffing is coming out and for stains. If a beloved pillow has either, or both, it is time for a new one.

Good money might have to be spent for a quality pillow, but think of it as a wise insurance policy for your health. To protect your investment, purchase pillowcases made of cotton or linen. Also, use an inner-zip-closure case to keep pillows clean. Experiment with some of these pillows to ease your back and neck.

Goose down travel pillow—This type of travel pillow rolls up, ties shut with attached ribbons, and fits neatly in a bag, briefcase, or suitcase.

Knee wedge pillow—This unique triangular-designed pillow elevates and supports knees to ease any strain on the back.

Maternity pillow—A maternity pillow will gently support the abdomen and lower back.

Accent pillows—Try out a supple leather pillow and watch it become even mellower with age. Accent pillows covered in brushed cotton, prewashed denim, or suede are all also guaranteed to please and are available in a variety of sizes and styles: round, square, Euro square, or boudoir.

Bolsters—These decorative pillows in an unusual shape of 6" x 15" or 8" x 20" are often placed on the bed for display. Why not break the norm and try them out as an all-over body support? Use a bolster to pillow the neck, an extra one to cushion the knees, and another to elevate the feet.

Bed reading chair—This wrap-around pillow chair offers back and arm support.

Featherbeds—Truly feel as if you are floating on a cloud with a featherbed at naptime when you lie on top of this pillow. Cover the bed, floor, or a daybed and expect the overall body warmth you would from a down comforter.

Body pillow—This large pillow provides comfort and support for the back and will hug you from head to toe.

MADAME RÉCAMIER
BY JACQUES LOUIS DAVID

CHAPTER TEN

Morpheus's Choices

PEACEFUL NAP SANCTUARIES

Time is what we want most but what we use the worst.
—William Penn (1644–1718)

Greek mythology claims the god of dreams, Morpheus, slept on a bed made entirely of ebony in a dim cave lit only by the brilliance of red poppies. While such legends may be an interesting story to read before a snooze, it does not offer good advice for what to nap upon or where to find solitude. Fortunately for modern woman, she can choose from an unlimited array of reclining seats, swings, and lounge chairs. Her toughest hurdle, though, will be finding the time to rest.

In surveys I conducted with women across the country, most believed that in order to achieve such bliss as an afternoon nap, they needed another hour in the day. But this is not so, according to recent medical studies. Any downtime, even a succinct ten-minute catnap, can revitalize the most harried or irritable individual and deliver peace of mind.

Other women note there is not a single place in their house where refuge can be found; the bathroom is not even safe. This is a long-standing truth in many American households. While the entire house may be considered a woman's terrain, there is nowhere to go to be completely alone.

MAKING SPACE

Abide in some place endlessly spacious,
Clear of trees, hills, habitations.
Thence comes the end of mind pressures.
—*from the ancient Sanskrit text,* Centering

In the 1960s, American anthropologist Edward T. Hall pioneered the study of proxemics—how we use space and react when someone invades our personal space. Findings showed that generally when someone steps into our space, in any form of this social altercation, a cathartic response is provoked. The heart races, while blood pressure, energy hormones, and adrenaline all surge—definitely not a good state for long-term health or a nap.

With the advent of the Industrial Age, historians have noted the development of "personal space" as a safeguard against the crush of humanity in cities and with four distinct zones defined. In the intimate zone, reserved for whispers and embraces, we permit lovers and immediate family within eighteen inches of our bodies. For close friends, any area from eighteen inches to four feet is acceptable. The social zone, four to ten feet is allowed for conversation with acquaintances. The public or strangers must stay outside the ten-foot circle.

Research shows that we need our space for our sanity. Artists have their art studios. Writers have their writing desks. Gardeners have their greenhouses. You, too, need a space to call your own, a private place to dream, collect your thoughts, and relax regularly. The importance of having a place where you can go and not be disturbed cannot be overemphasized.

Think about what area of your home can be converted into a serene and private place. Consider all rooms—from the attic to the library—even if it is only a temporary setup like the sofa in the formal parlor or the patio swing when the weather breaks. Rearrange bedroom furniture and claim a corner with an oversized stuffed chair and a matching ottoman or add a chaise longue with a small side table. The playroom, bathroom, or the nook under the stairs filled with gift wrap and boxes—all could make a splendid and private sanctuary.

A Room with a Bed

When I do nap, it is on the couch…less guilt since it appears accidental that way.

—*Joni Souverein, mother, Draper, Utah*

Feng Shui is the Japanese belief that how a house, office, or room is designed and decorated can affect one's health, wealth, and life.

According to the ancient art of feng shui, the bedroom is considered to be the most *yin* room of the house and is meant to be small in scale, represent darkness and silence, and be filled with soothing textures. Most bedrooms today are designed to be the complete opposite. With areas for a wide screen television, gym equipment, and a built-in desk, the large suite is usually decorated in the color white, which includes the linens, drapery, and carpeting as well as the twenty-foot high walls. Be brave and deviate from white. Paint your new nap room in hues of blues and greens, associated with peace, healing, and the colors of the earth.

For better sleep, sleep scientists advocate a firmer mattress and stress the importance of rotating the mattress from top to bottom one month and then right to left in the next thirty days. Check to see if the foundation piece has multiple torsion bars and strong support beams to prevent bowing in the middle of the bed. Do not use the space underneath the bed as storage; allow air to circulate. This investment will last longer than your linens, curtains, carpeting, and appliances. Be a smart sleep shopper and buy the best mattress you can afford.

Around A.D. *750, the idea of sleeping in a bed finally became popular throughout France and Germany.*

The guest room, an underused room, would make a pleasant retreat on a daily basis. Make a sign for the door with the French expression: *Chambre des Amis*, "Room of Friends," and decide to be the pampered guest at this lovely bed-and-breakfast inn. In a cedar trunk, store a music collection of relaxing sounds, a few Euro square and neck roll pillows, a goose down comforter, and a bottle of heavenly room spray. All of theses luxurious items, necessary and preferred by European royalty and guests of five-star hotels, can be kept here just for you.

For sleep-inducing fragrances in the bedroom, try lavender,
chamomile, and jasmine to pacify the mind and body.

ISLAND OF INDULGENCE

Far too many people, conscientious, ambitious and hardworking, won't, for
whatever reason, give themselves permission to have a moment's peace.
—*Alexandra Stoddard (b. 1941)*

For the summer months, create your own island of indulgence outside. Move a daybed out onto the porch. Arrange a mosquito net canopy around the four corners of this designated nap haven. On other days, open all the windows and toss a fluffy rug on the floor.

Lie on the floor with your feet rolled out and your palms open to the sky. Close your eyes and visualize small waves lapping at the edge of a white sand beach very far away. White stucco buildings with brightly painted indigo doors are stacked all over the hillsides. Continue to daydream of the sun-drenched isle, and after traipsing around the narrow streets in your mind, you might believe you are there.

Another island for indulgence to ponder is the library, den, or great room. Libraries, a by-product from the Age of Reason, became very popular when it was considered fashionable to own many books. During the eighteenth century, both social gatherings and private study took place here in the home's most elegant room.

In our era of multimedia centers acceptable as a regular fixture in most households, do your part to bring back a literary piece of the logical past and build a library as your napping retreat. Add a bookshelf in the den or great room or simply surround yourself with books stacked on the floor, tables, and counters. Include a small table for a beverage and a scented candle and squeeze a comfortable chair near the window or under a good lamp. Soon, you might find others in your household asking for time in your spot away from the televisions and computers.

If a room in your house is not available, design your new nap spot within a busy room and turn ordinary spots into extraordinary ones. Lavish essentials will easily transform any room into a temporary relaxation spot. Clear a shelf or cabinet to keep snooze-inducing items together and encourage frequent stops to nurture mind, body, and spirit.

On a super-busy day, cover the couch with a silk sheet and curl up into a delicious sleep, or fill up a window seat with various pillows to doze away for half an hour, surrounded in deluxe comfort. At other times, roll out a yoga mat or a thick comforter and gently sink into the ground. When you awaken, just leave all the stress on the floor.

In the home office, consider a daybed. Instead of using the bottom as a second bed, fill the drawer with pillows, blankets, books, music, and aromatherapy treats such as a diffuser or a light bulb ring. This new spot can also be a comfortable thinking area when you are not snoozing.

Dress up a garden shed and move in or decorate the walled patio for a new place to pull thoughts together or pause in the day. Find solace in the abundance of blooming buds and natural daylight. Sit beneath the canopy of a beloved tree and do nothing for a while.

ADD BEAUTY TO LIFE

One of the secrets to a happy life is continuous small treats.
—Iris Murdoch (1919–1999)

Weekends were made for naps. First thing Saturday morning, set up your private sanctuary with all the extra touches that you would include for a best friend. Afterward, watch as the weekend unfolds to be a better one just knowing that your spot is ready and waiting for you.

Everything in your space should add to your sense of well-being and foster peaceful contemplation. Keep your sanctuary uncluttered. Piles of mail, clothes, and paperwork will induce feelings of stress and whatever is viewed before drifting off to sleep will leave a lasting impression. Illuminated clocks can also distract and clock-watching leads to anxiety. Hide the desk clock or your watch, but set a trusty alarm to insure that you that will be back at the job after your power nap.

Display spiritual or emotional items in your new corner of tranquillity. Choose only a few cherished items to grace this area: an heirloom, photo, memento of a trip, or a child's work of art. Look for serene colors, elegant shapes, and interesting objects with intriguing textures to place near you. Nature is a good place to discover something unique for your nap room. Position one of the objects of beauty close by so you can focus on it upon waking

HOLD EVERYTHING

Showcase your essential nap accessories to remind yourself to enjoy the peaceful time that you have waiting for you each day. Store your linens in a fragrant cedar chest or one made of sturdy, solid maple. Any type of chest can serve double-duty as a bench in a bedroom, hallway, office, or as a table behind a couch. Along a tall wall, a wooden ladder can attractively display your nap blankets. Make beautiful throws easily accessible on an ornate wrought iron or cherry wood rack or to hold quilts and pillows, fill and stack several wooden crates in the corner. Capture all of your robes and nightgowns on a coat rack to make it easy to change into one after lunch.

Keep nap essentials together in handy containers and think outside the typical box, basket, or tray. On the corner of the guest bed, leave a silver or other fancy tray with a book of poems, a teacup and saucer, and a decorative glass bowl of potpourri to remind you of your nap later in the day.

Use an ottoman as a low table on which to set a wooden tray with a thick book, a mug of hot chocolate topped with whipped cream, and a vanilla bean-scented candle. Add a flannel blanket to reserve a chair and transform any room into a one-room cabin. On a coffee table, place a black lacquer Japanese tray with a glazed teapot, cup, fortune cookies, *The Book of Tea*, and a small Zen sand garden to still the mind before a nap.

Wooden magazine butlers with carrying handles usually only store old magazines, but why not recycle and use this convenient container for nap essentials? Hatboxes can house affordable luxuries and decorate an open shelf. Big, wicker laundry baskets with hardy handles provide ample space for a folded quilt, an herbal eye cover, meditative music, and chenille slippers.

Each month, change your nap ingredients to try something new and renew your appreciation of this solitary time. Load up a fruit crate with nap essentials necessary to greet spring on the porch. For summertime naps, fill a steel pail to accompany you outdoors. Carry a brimming wooden wine box full of comforting items outside on autumn afternoons.

A PLACE IN NATURE

The sun shines not on us, but in us. The rivers flow not past,
but through us, thrilling, tingling, vibrating every fiber and
cell of the substance of our bodies, making them glide and sing.
—John Muir (1838–1914)

When the weather changes, it is time to reconsider the perfect nap spot and move outdoors. Follow the sun and test out the porch, patio, or balcony. Hammocks are synonymous with relaxation in all cultures and in any language. Take a hint from Alcibiades, one of Socrates's students credited by scholars with the invention of the hammock, and find the answer to the pressing question of where to nap outdoors.

In the late fifteenth century, Christopher Columbus discovered the West Indies and natives napping in their rope beds. Today in Brazil, beachgoers lounge in colorful slings stretched between palm trees. For more than a hundred years, Pawley's Island, South Carolina, has been renowned for its hammocks. Its first 100 percent cotton twill bed was reportedly made for a sea captain who claimed that sleeping in the hull was too hot.

An experienced weaver can create approximately eighty hammocks in a forty-hour week.

The current marketplace is filled with all types of hammock to try. If you prefer to be coddled and swaddled, pick a hammock that fits the body like a cocoon. To stretch out, choose a hammock with wooden stave stretchers which keep the bed open. A bit of balance is required to enter and exit the latter, but either choice guarantees a blissful nap. A handcrafted, crocheted cotton-rope hammock with all of its old-fashioned styling—tassels, wooden balls, and decorative scalloped edge—will be as much a treasure to lounge in as it is to admire.

While your intention to bring the hammock into the house after each napping session may be good, it will be soon forgotten, so make sure the wood of the stretchers is sealed with a weather-resistant marine varnish. Cypress, oak, and teak are wise selections and can be treated to retain the honey-golden color. Make afternoons even more luxurious with the addition of a few hammock accessories. To prevent sunburn, think about a full-size canopy. For extra comfort, add a hammock pillow and a quilted pad. For convenience's sake, select a small table of teak, cypress, or other durable material to hold everything your respite requires.

Another option to consider for outside contentment is a hammock chair. This cotton rope chair can be hung from the porch rafters, a strong tree branch, or inside on an exposed beam. For complete comfort, you might also want to order custom-made pillows for your new nap seat.

If the backyard trees are not ready to accommodate an adult swinging in the wind, an enamel frame made of heavy-gauge steel is your solution to outdoor sleeping. With the purchase of a hammock stand, mobility is gained—now napping can take place anywhere, inside or out, and away on a vacation. This summer, justify the costs of a hammock by claiming "peace of mind" and when the bare trees are outlined against a dark, gray sky, bring a taste of the garden indoors and string up your trusty hammock in the den. Your investment will be put to good use year-round.

BE A DIVA

I love and accept myself just the way I am.
—Louise L. Hay (b.1926)

In opulent parlors all throughout Europe, Victorian ladies swooned and fainted on chaise longue chairs. Current-day applications of these truly voluptuous seats are now set aside for naps. With a reclining low section and its back rising ever so slightly, this relaxation chair is a heavenly escape here on Earth. The framing of such recliners are as varied as its owners; select from wrought iron, cherry, pine, oak, or rattan.

Rattan, sometimes called wicker, is the catch-all name for a group of vine-like palms, which includes the water hyacinth plant, growing prominently in Asia. Every summer, fishermen must harvest these water plants to keep them from choking the Mekong River, a waterway flowing twenty-six hundred miles along the plateau of Tibet. In Thailand, the water hyacinth reeds are dried and softened before being woven by hand to make natural chaise longues, chair and ottoman sets, tables, and other matching furniture.

Wicker furniture was first discovered in King Tutankhamen's tomb, but only first arrived in the United States by way of the *Mayflower* for baby Peregrine White's woven cradle. In the Gadabout car's short production from 1914 to 1915, the passenger's seats were made of wicker. Later in the twentieth century, the familiar, thick Sears Roebuck catalogs offered fancy wicker furniture collections like those that adorned celebrity houses and affluent manors such as the Vanderbilt home. Movies and books based in the colonial Far East conjure up images of rain-drenched tropics and swelteringly hot days. Many residences built for the British had covered porches and exquisite garden rooms to offer protection for the expatriates who were not accustomed to the extremes in weather.

Today, rattan furniture still offers an invitation to sit back and relax, no matter what the weather decides to do. Now, armed with such wicker trivia, consider the purchase of a rattan chaise longue an environmental good deed indeed.

Cleaning Tip: Once or twice a year, vacuum the dust off wicker furniture. With a painted finish, mist with water and wipe with a rag or a sponge. Natural, unfinished wicker can be restored to its original sheen after dusting it with lemon or linseed oil.

NAPPING AS ART

Mostly we're too busy living to stop and notice we're alive.
—Neil Gaiman (b. 1960)

Teak benches, a permanent fixture in English gardens for more than a century, still grace public parks and make an ideal sitting choice in any tranquil garden. Teak is simply the finest and most stable timber available for extended outside use. As a true testimony to the test of time and adverse weather conditions, this wood has been long used in the marine industry. It is a dense wood, rich in oil, and almost impervious to rotting, splitting, or buckling. Position a cushioned bench among the flowers as Claude Monet did at Giverny, France, to be ready for a summertime nap any afternoon.

Sweet living is when you can slow down to a Sunday's pace on a Wednesday and a rocking chair or glider can help make this transition possible. Throughout the Appalachians, the original ladder-back rocking chairs still line the front porches of many country stores and inns.

Take another step back in time with the addition of a porch glider. Succumb to the glider's tall back and wide arms as you sink into its cushioned seat. Wrap yourself up in a blanket, rock gently, and set your breathing to its rhythmic music as it creaks to and fro.

When you find yourself looking out the window mid morning wishing it were time for your afternoon nap, a garden swing might be a wise addition to the yard this summer. Suspended from a mature tree branch and padded with a three-inch thick pillow, your new nap swing will sway your tired body gracefully above the ground.

In the garden, poolside, or on the patio, you can count on most outdoor furniture to combine form with function in ergonomically contoured backrests, adjustable reclining levels, a hidden drink tray, a multiple-position footrest, and locking wheels to move you in or out of the sun—all give you the exact pampering you deserve.

Choose chair pads and pillows in the color green, the universal symbol for nature and freshness, and add comfort to both the body and spirit. Choices for the right nap chair are endless, but always apply the touch principle, this time with your whole body. Looks can be deceiving, so let your sense of touch make the final call.

RETURN TO THE MOUNTAINS

The real voyage of discovery consists not in seeking new landscapes but in having new eyes.

—Marcel Proust (1871–1922)

The Adirondack Wilderness, with more than three thousand lakes and thirty thousand miles of rivers, is the home of the great American chair—the Adirondack. This classic relaxation chair with its deep-angled seat and generous arms is available with a footrest and matching companion side table to ensure all is within reach. If adding to your outdoor furniture collection, look at other Adirondack designs, which include a rocking chair and loveseat version.

Reminiscent of hunting and fishing lodges, northern Maine cedar chairs are made from twigs cut while still green and flexible. Artisans bend and twist cedar twigs to create one-of-a-kind works of art in the form of beautiful, comfortable chairs. The big advantage to the purchase of this type of nap chair is that there is no need to weatherproof this natural furniture.

Cedar log furniture is another handsome option for outdoor use. As rustic as the wilderness, cedar can be treated as part of nature, which translates into easy maintenance. The splits and cracks in the logs, caused naturally by the moisture escaping from the green logs and shrinkage of the cellular structure of the log, do not weaken the structure of your furniture. Cedar is resistant to rot and insect damage, so be assured of many years of enjoyment. Less expensive than teak, cedar will weather to a similar natural shade of silvery-gray. Choose from a single chair, a double chair with an adorning table, or a yard swing.

Cleaning Tip: *To treat, wipe the wood with a clean rag and rubbing alcohol. Natural tannins in the cedar will protect the furniture from insects and mildew.*

SUMMER DAYS FOREVER

Cliffs, fountains, rivers, seasons, times—let all remind the soul of heaven.
—William Wordsworth (1770–1850)

As the summer days fade away to autumn, linger outside longer with a chimenea, or fireplace. For more than two hundred and fifty years, the Indians of Mexico used these unique, fired-kiln ovens made of clay for heat and cooking. Handcrafted by artisans, these freestanding pear-shaped fire pits are great for a party for one. The wood fire, contained on three sides, can still warm your toes with its small, safe opening in the front.

SECRETS OF PEACE

If everyday is an awakening, you will never grow old, you will just keep growing.
—Gail Sheehy (b.1937)

The key to making time is to seize time. You must consciously live in the moment when attempting to take a nap or to carve out a few minutes for yourself. Think of nothing else except what you are enjoying. Practice in small sessions of time at the office or at home. This deliberate slowness, a pausing of time, is required to truly feel, taste, hear, see, and smell life again. Indulge in a few acts of time preservation this week. Try any of these suggestions and savor these little stolen moments of time.

A WEEK OF SELF-CARE GIFTS

You have to take the time to live. Living takes time.
—*Eleanor McMillen Brown (1890–1992)*

Monday

Place one of your favorite flowers in your best vase, a small topiary of rosemary or another aromatic herb, in an area where you will see it for most of the day. Stop and smell this intoxicating aroma full of life at least three times during the day.

If children are at home with you during the day, play in the dirt together. Plant a fragrant dwarf orange tree, a strawberry plant, or any vegetable for cleaner air tomorrow and the hope of a harvest. Close your eyes, feel the soil between your fingers, and smell the grounding scent of the earth. Visit your plant throughout the week to check if watering is necessary.

Tuesday

Throw an impromptu tea party for yourself and the little ones or a neighbor. Set a small table with a teapot and everyday mugs, paper plates, party napkins, sugar cubes, cookies, and milk. Have everyone talk about dreams of the future.

If you must go off to the office today, carefully wrap a small teapot and a fine china teacup in a dishtowel, which can be used later as a mini tablecloth. In your afternoon relaxation bag, add a few honey sticks, a tin canister of various tea bags, and a couple of musical selections by a classical composer. At 2:30 P.M., slip the CD into the computer, sit back, and sip an herbal infusion. Listen while a symphony plays peaceful sounds for you and deliberately let go of twenty minutes.

Wednesday

Pack a lavender-scented dream pillow or other small pillow plus a portable sound machine to take with you to the office. Tell your boss that you are planning an energy revival over a late lunch today. After you eat, close the door and turn off the lights, phone, and pager. Take off your shoes and elevate your feet. Schedule a half-hour appointment with yourself and be there. If the office lights are too distracting to nap while at work, try a sleep mask or dark fabric to block the windows or the rim of the door. Blackout shades, sometimes used in hotels, are also available to aid the light sensitive.

If working from home either on housework or paperwork, make a relaxation spot before your day starts. On the corner of the bed, set up a breakfast tray with a fancy glass and an ice bucket to hold a bottle of sparkling mineral water. Mark a book at the passage to read and place on top of an incredibly, soft blanket. Complete this tranquil setting and toss a few extra pillows on the bed. Close the door, but promise to return this afternoon for a half-hour respite.

Thursday

Let the meditative music of an Andean flute and a *pakawaj,* a double-headed Indian classical drum, fill the air. Watch its effect on the children or business associates, depending on who is down the hall.

Sit for a while and be still. Truly hear the poignant melody. Slowly, its rhythm fills your mind's ear and provides a soothing background, which will continue to play for you during the rest of the day.

Friday

After breakfast, toss a Mexican blanket, a handmade quilt, or another favorite throw on the living room sofa and reserve the room for an afternoon siesta. A few photos arranged on the coffee table will help you move mentally into a peaceful place later at naptime.

At your office desk, block out twenty minutes on your daily calendar to indulge in a short, yet effective, spa break. Bring a small hand towel and a flip-top bottle of sweet almond carrier oil mixed with the essence of jasmine. Remove your rings, bracelets, and watch. Sit back and elevate your feet.

During your well-deserved hand massage, play soft jazz music. Massage the oil into the palm of your hands, on each knuckle, all finger pads, and each wrist. Repeat the massage on your other hand. Close your eyes. Pay attention to the relaxing essence and music as your mind and body begins to relax.

Weekends

If the weather permits, venture outside. Hang a hammock between the trees and let a breeze rock you to sleep or spread a huge beach towel on the grass. If the family decides to join you, load up the porch or patio furniture with extra pillows, blankets, and books and designate the hour as "Quiet time."

NAP WELL AND OFTEN

Wheresoever you go, go with all your heart.

—*Confucius (551–479 B.C.)*

You need this time to be still. The secret is to start with little steps and make the small things count. Stimulate your five senses, once again. Appreciate colors found in nature and the silky touch of a blanket. Enjoy the wonderful aroma of new foods and beverages; listen to beautiful sounds or the songs of nature. When you pay extra attention to yourself, your mind and body will experience a new sensation of being alive.

How and where you choose to relax and nap will be a personal decision, one that will work within your daily life. Some women rest every day, others put aside two lovely hours on Saturdays. Many sleep, a few meditate, and others daydream in their time alone, yet all achieve the same peaceful results. Be patient with yourself, but be generous as well. Find the time and a place for you to be with only you. This is truly what your spirit needs and deserves.

Still Life with Books
By Tammy Valley

Books

RECOMMENDED READINGS

I hoard books. They are people who do not leave.
—Anne Sexton (1928–1974)

In the research for this book about naps and my discovery of finding time for myself, I found many wonderful books. Listed here are suggested readings if you are interested in learning more about a particular subject or would like to have a worthy companion for your quiet time.

AROMATHERAPY

A book is like a garden carried in the pocket.

—*Arab proverb*

Aromatherapy for Women and Children: Pregnancy and Childbirth by Jane Dye

A Natural History of the Senses by Diane Ackerman

The Art of Sensual Aromatherapy by Nitya Lacroix

The Backyard Medicine Chest: An Herbal Primer by Douglas Schar

The Essential Aromatherapy Book by Carole McGilvery and Jimi Reed

The Healing Herbs: The Ultimate Guide to the Curative Power of Nature's Medicine by Michael Castleman

BOOKS OF COMFORT

The book should be a ball of light in one's hand.

—*Ezra Pound (1885–1972)*

A Room of Her Own by Chris Casson Madden

Creating a Charmed Life: Spiritual Secrets Every Busy Woman Should Know by Victoria Moran

Living a Beautiful Life by Alexandra Stoddard

Living Organic: Easy Steps to an Organic Family Lifestyle by Adrienne Clarke, Helen Porter, Helen
Quested, and Patricia Thomas

Penhaligon's Scented Treasury of Verse and Prose: The Language of Flowers by Shelia Pickles

Sensual Home by Illse Crawford

Simple Pleasures: Soothing Suggestions and Small Comforts for Living Well Year Round by Robert Taylor,
Susannah Seton, and David Greer

Take Time for Your Life: A Personal Coach's Seven Step Program for Creating the Life You Want by Cheryl
Richardson

The Art of Doing Nothing: Simple Ways to Make Time for Yourself by Veronique Vienne

A Book of Bliss: Thoughts to Make You Smile, Sourcebooks

The Comfort Queen's Guide to Life: Create All That You Need with Just What You've Got by Jennifer Louden

Zen Style Balance and Simplicity for Your Home by Jane Tidbury

BEVERAGES

Some books are to be tasted, others to be swallowed and some few to be chew and digested.

—*Francis Bacon (1561–1626)*

Icy Concoctions

Smoothies and Juices by Ed Marquard

Smoothies, Shakes and Frappes: 750 Refreshing Revitalizing and Nourishing Drinks by Sally Ann Berk

Super Smoothies: 50 Recipes for Health and Energy by Mary Corpening Barber and Sara Corpening Whiteford

Tea and other Hot Drinks

Aromatic Teas and Herbal Infusions by Laura Fronty

French Tea: The Pleasures of the Table by Carole Manchester

If Teacups Could Talk: Sharing a Cup of Kindness with Treasured Friends by Emilie Barnes

The Book of Coffee and Tea: A Guide to the Appreciation of Fine Coffees, Teas and Herbal Beverages by Joel Schapira

The Book of Tea by Kakuoa Okakura

The Tea Lover's Companion: The Ultimate Connoisseur's Guide to Buying, Brewing and Enjoying Tea by James Norwood Pratt

RELAXATION BOOKS

Fear less, hope more,

eat less, chew more,

whine less, breathe more,

talk less, say more,

love more and

all good things will be yours.

——*Swedish proverb*

Massage

5-Minute Massage: Quick and Simple Exercises to Reduce Tension and Stress by Robert Thé

Acupressure for Everybody by Cathryn Bauer

Acupressure for Women by Cathryn Bauer

Learn to Relax by Mike George

Massage for Beginners by Marilyn Aslani

Meditation and Creative Guided Imagery

A Thousand Paths to Enlightenment by David Baird

A Path with Heart: A Guide through the Perils and Promises of Spiritual Life by Jack Kornfield

Being Nobody, Going Nowhere by Ayya Khema

Don't Just Do Something, Sit There by Sylvia Boorstein

Everyday Serenity: Meditation for People Who Do Too Much by David Kundtz

Going on Being: Buddhism and the Way of Change: A Positive Psychology for the West by Mark Epstein

Guided Imagery by Larry Moen

Instructions to the Cook: A Zen Master's Lesson in Living a Life that Matters by Bernard Glassman and Rick Fields

In the Lap of Buddha by Cavin Harrison

Simple Zen: A Guide to Living Moment by Moment by C. Alexander Simpkins, Ph.D. and Annellen Simpkins, Ph.D.

Stumbling toward Enlightenment by Geri Larkin

The Art of Happiness: A Handbook for Living by His Holiness the Dala Lama, Howard C. Cutler, M.D., and Grove Gardner

The Long Road Turns to Joy: A Guide to Walking Meditation by Thich Nhat Hanh and Robert Aitken

The Inner Art of Meditation by Jack Kornfield

The Power of Positive Choices: Adding and Subtracting Your Way to a Great Life by Gail McMeekin

What is Meditation? Meditation for Everyone by Rob Nairn

Wherever You Go, There You Are: Mindfulness Meditation in Everyday Life by Jon Kabat-Zinn

Zen and the Art of Well-Being by Eric Chaline

Zen Mind, Beginner's Mind by Shunryu Suzuki

Sleep

The Promise of Sleep: A Pioneer in Sleep Medicine Explores the Vital Connection between Health, Happiness and a Good Night's Sleep by William C. Dement M.D., Ph.D.

Power Sleep: The Revolutionary Program that Prepares Your Mind for Peak Performance by Dr. James B. Maas

Sleep Thieves: An Eye-Opening Exploration into the Science and Mysteries of Sleep by Stanley Coren

Yoga

Office Yoga: Simple Stretches for Busy People by Darrin Zeer

Yoga Builds Bones: Easy, Gentle Stretches that Prevent Osteoporosis by Jan Maddern

Yoga for Busy People: Increase Energy and Reduce Stress in Minutes a Day by Dawn Groves

Yoga: The Spirit and Practice of Moving into Stillness by Erich Schiffmann

Permissions

p. xi *Beginner's Mind* by Amy Murphy. Reprinted by permission of the artist.

p. xiv *Asleep among the Foxgloves* by Sidney Shelton (fl. 1881-89) Waterhouse and Dodd, London, UK/Bridgeman Art Library.

p. 10 *Girl under a Parasol* by Pedro Lira (1850-fl.1872-1901) Whitford and Hughes, London, UK/Bridgeman Art Library.

p. 16 *The Soul of the Rose*, 1908 (oil on canvas) by John William Waterhouse (1849-1917) Private Collection/Julian Hartnoll, London, UK/Bridgeman Art Library.

p. 26 *The Betrothed*, 1892 (oil on canvas) by John William Godward (1861-1922) Guildhall Art Gallery, Corporation of London, UK/Bridgeman Art Library.

p. 42 *Expectations*, 1900 by John William Godward © Manchester City Art Galleries.

p. 60 *Peace Rose* by K.S. Robischon. Reprinted by permission of the artist.

p. 68 *Geranium Peltatum* by Curtis Botanical Illustrations, 1700–1900 Antique Prints.

p. 88 *Sweet Sounds*, 1918 by John William Godward (1861-1922) Roy Miles Fine Paintings/ Bridgeman Art Library.

p. 104 *Girl Reading*, 1878 by Charles Edward Perugini © Manchester City Art Galleries.

p. 128 *Noon-Day Rest*, 1910 (oil on canvas) by John William Godward (1861-1922) Private Collection, Bridgeman Art Library.

p. 146 *Madame Récamier*, 1800 (oil on canvas) by Jaques Louis David (1748-1825) Louvre, Paris, France/Giraudon-Bridgeman Art Library.

p. 166 *Still Life with Books* by Tammy Valley. Reprinted by permission of the artist.

ABOUT THE AUTHOR

Jill Murphy Long is a certified yoga instructor, athlete, ski instructor, and professional writer. Her background is in advertising. She held the positions of partner and creative director/copywriter for ten years at Murphy & Watt Advertising Agency and The Ad Group and prior to that she worked for Foote, Cone, and Belding, *Adweek*, and the Advertising Center. She has organized and led several weekly writers' groups and is a founding member of The Rancho Reading Club. She holds a B.A. in Communications with an emphasis in Marketing from California State University–Fullerton, has traveled extensively in all of the fifty United States, and has lived abroad. She currently resides in Steamboat Springs, Colorado, with her husband Greg and daughter Brittany Christine.